I ROMANCED THE STONE

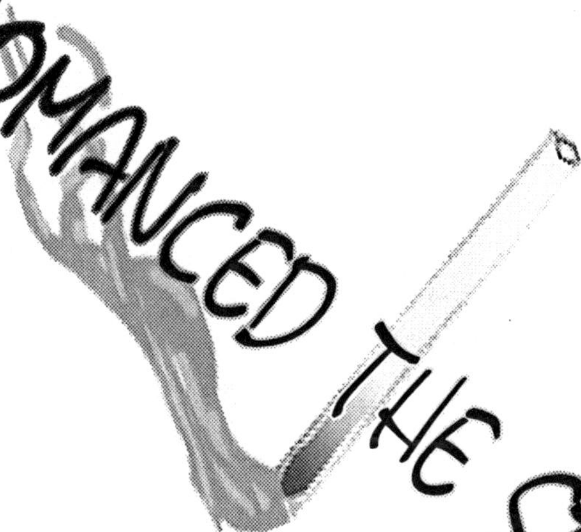

This is a factual account of events happening to the author however all names and locations have been changed to protect the identiy of any people he may mention.

ISBN: 0-9779680-3-0
Library of Congress Control Number: 2006931114
Published by Global Authors Publications

Filling the GAP in publishing

Edited by Barbara Sachs Sloan
Interior Design by KathleenWalls
Cover Design by Kathleen Walls
Front Cover Art by T.C. McMullen

Printed in USA for Global Authors Publications

I ROMANCED THE STONE

(MEMOIRS OF A RECOVERING HIPPIE)

AN AUTOBIOGRAPHICAL TRUE STORY

BY

MARVIN D. WILSON

DEDICATION

This book is dedicated to (and in loving memory of) my father. His spirit lives on in me, and throughout my entire family, and even though he never lived to read this book, I know that now, in me, he is well pleased.

THANKSGIVING

I would like to express my thankfulness to all of my wonderful family. To my wife, whose depth of love, compassion, acceptance and forgiveness, is beyond all measure by any normal spousal standards; to my children, who rallied together in love and concern, who reached out to me, and took me by the hand, and pulled me up to safe ground, when I was hanging by a couple of fingers on a faulted precipice; to my father, who, although not with us any more in body, still lives on in our lives as a greater-than-life force of spirituality and guidance, and, I believe, who is watching over us all, lovingly, every day of our lives; to my mother, the never-ending source of love, who nurtured me with that love as a child, and who continues to do so today, and who continues to lead this family, as the consummate spiritual elder.

Thanksgiving to all my brothers. They stood by me, judged me not, and helped in every way possible, to insure that their older brother would be made whole again. Thanks to all my sisters-in-law, uncles and aunts, all the cousins, nieces, nephews, friends of the family, and so on, who said a prayer for Marvin when they were informed that the old maverick was at it again, this time worse than ever before.

And in closing, I want to say a very special "Thank You!" to my brother Dana and sister-in-law Kim. They took me in and nursed me back to life when I was staring into the abyss of my tortured and damned soul.

PREFACE

A crackhead wrote this book. *This story had to be written by a drug addict;* even before I went in for rehabilitation, I knew that much, for two reasons. The first reason was I intuited it as a necessary ingredient in the healing process, at least for someone like myself, who has always been a journal keeper, a writer about life experiences, and a reflective person at heart. I figure things out by writing about them. One of the imperative provisions for me, with respect to a suitable rehab facility, was whether or not they offered their clients any "free time" and would allow them to have a word processor to be able to write about their experiences *during* recovery.

I also knew I was going to conquer my narcotics addiction, at any and all costs; this was not optional in my mind or in my heart of hearts. I would either get clean and be made whole again, or die trying. I was absolutely determined and committed that there was to be no turning back. I couldn't live any longer as the person I had become. Whenever I spoke to an intake counselor at any of the facilities I contacted, my attitude, I heard repeatedly, was the best thing I had going for me, because (they all said) without that *intense desire* on the part of the client to be healed, the failure rate was much higher, and the relapse rate much, much higher.

God has always spoken to me, from as early as I can remember. I have not always called that little intuitive "good" voice God, but I've always heard it. I knew it was smart, smarter and much wiser than me. When I finally gave in to this voice of God, summoned my demons into court, and managed, somehow, to let them know that I intended to have them executed immediately, and without trial or hope of reinstatement, I knew I was going into battle. This was a battle between good and evil, and the prize was life or death. I was ready to fight.

And this battle *had* to be written about!

Even in my lowly, confused, agonized, cracked-up head at the time, I heard that admonition from God as clearly as I hear the clicking of my keyboard right now as I write. Which leads to the second reason for the necessity of writing this story. I resolved that if nothing else, my terrible mistakes, my horrid atrocities against myself, my family, and everything that is good and righteous in this world, would at least be recompensed in some measure by writing this true story, so others could read about it. It was my hope they could gain enough pertinent knowledge, wisdom and *fear* to avert making, or allowing anyone dear to them to make, the same mistakes I made. It was to be my way of making a bad thing good, one possibly redeeming facet of a horrible subject matter, that being my life as a crackhead.

I made it through to recovery and cure. I wrote about it, all of it, and here it is. Neither you, nor anyone else dear to you, need go through what I have. For as you will read, not everyone, in fact, almost no one, is as fortunate as I was. My advice to anyone even *flirting* with the idea of sampling a dangerously addictive narcotic like crack cocaine? ***NEVER TAKE THAT FIRST HIT!*** Read chapters seven and eight of this book first, and then think long and hard about it. Then pray that you never go my way.

I asked my new-found friend, my sister-in-law, my counselor, therapist and spiritual guide in time of need, Pastor Kimberly Linn Wilson, to compose some words at the end of my story. I did so because I felt it would be enlightening to the reader to hear, from her perspective, just what a monumental challenge it is to assist someone through rehabilitation from a serious addiction. Even when the patient wants to be cured, it requires an effort that few people can muster alone. It makes the miracle of full and lasting cure just that much more miraculous. It not only takes skill, it takes love, it requires tenacity and fortitude, and, I agree with her now: It needs God in the mix, too, as a basic and fundamental ingredient. Through her short story, you will see me and my struggle, along with her own struggle, and the two of us growing together symbiotically in divine wisdom, through a pair of different eyes.

CONTENTS

Chapter One:	Getting My Work on the Way to Work	Page 1
Chapter Two:	There Once Was a Happy Hippie	Page 6
Chapter Three:	"Just Say No" -- Are You Kidding Me?	Page 12
Chapter Four:	Growing Up and Getting Straight	Page 19
Chapter Five:	The Unhappy Yuppie	Page 23
Chapter Six:	The Good Guy Turns Bad and Gets Ugly	Page 28
Chapter Seven:	The Betrayal of Gibson	Page 47
Chapter Eight:	"Picking Up" on the Romance	Page 57
Chapter Nine:	This is All Just a Bad Dream, Right?	Page 68
	Part 1: The Internal Dialogue	page 68
	Part 2: Trying to Wake Up	page 71
	Part 3: The Last Curtain Call	page 87
Chapter Ten:	The Road to Recovery	Page 92
Chapter Eleven:	Patience	Page 103
Chapter Twelve:	The Work Ahead	Page 109
Epilogue:		Page 115
The Counselor's Perspective:	(a postlude by Kim Wilson)	Page 121
Bibliography:		Page 131

CHAPTER ONE:

GETTING MY WORK ON THE WAY TO WORK

Already late for my job, I run into a local seedy party store, rush up to the counter, and impatiently get in line behind a slender blonde I've seen prostituting around the area. I suspect she's a junkie, as I observe her fidgeting, scratching at her neck, face, and arms, and pulling nervously at her stringy, unwashed hair. She gets her pop and smokes, and staggers out toward the front door, chanting some unintelligible hip-hop song. I step up, telling the young clerk, "Give me 'the works,' dog." He gives me this knowing look and proceeds to fill a small paper bag with a "rose stem" (thin glass tube), "char" (a "Chore Boy" copper scouring pad) and several cigarette lighters. "That's six bucks, homes," the boyish-looking Chicano says, handing the bag to me. I pay him, walk out the back door, scanning the parking lot for any heat, hop in my car, and head around the corner, where I've got my pick-up all set.

I pull into the parking lot of a project complex. There's litter everywhere and a rankling bouquet of garbage, stale beer, and urine wafting through the air, emanating from the overflowing dumpster enclosure at the far end. It's a warm, smelly, sunny day, here in the ghetto, and in the center of the courtyard there's a pickup game of hoops going on, a bunch of gangsta-looking street-ballers, talking smack and showboating. I see my dealer, a tall, heavily built African American, with deep-set black eyes, standing there in a Michael Jordan jumpsuit, waiting on me. Our eyes contact; he makes a subtle hand motion, indicating the best parking spot for me to take. I turn the car around and back into the space, so I can watch for any unwanted characters approaching my vehicle. He glances side to side, then saunters toward the car. Opening the side door, he sits down, and says, "Half a buck, right?" I reply, "Yep," and he drops a small plastic bag in my hand. I give him the fifty dollars; he gets out, suggesting, "If you need me later, I'll be around here all day." "Holla atcha this afternoon, dog," I shout at him, while pulling out of the parking lot, breathing a sigh of relief. I'm well aware that this place is hot, constantly under surveillance by cops, undercover narcs, and often frequented by thugs who will mug and rob a white dude who obviously has enough money to own a car.

Now I'm getting happy. I've got everything I need to get high, and once again, I've made a clean pick-up, with no heat and no trouble.

With a big smiley face, I drive to a nearby strip mall and park in an inconspicuous spot on the outskirts of the lot, again backing in so I can keep a watch on the entire area. After a couple of eye scans, I pull out the paper bag and begin preparing my heater. I take out my old stem, which has been burnt down to about one inch long (it started out four inches long). The familiar candied-acrid smell of it heightens my anticipation. Using a narrow pen I always carry with me, gently I push out the old blackened char, letting it fall on my lap.

I pull the Chore Boy pad out of the bag, and using the razor blade (that's also always with me), I cut free a narrow strip of the copper wire mesh and twist it into a thin rope, about two inches long. I test the lighters to see which one has the most firepower, and using that one, I sear the copper rope until it burns off the chemical coating and turns a medium brown color. The burning gives off a rancid odor that would repulse most people, but it comforts me. Then, after carefully twisting a little bit of the old char into the new, I insert the perfectly prepped stuff into one end of the new stem. Using my "pusher" (the pen that is narrow enough to slide inside the glass tube), I push and tamp it back and forth a few times, until it is compacted to about one inch long and fits snugly inside the heater. Finally, positioning it about a quarter inch down from one end of the stem, leaving space for my first load, my brand new heater is ready; and I'm a happy crackhead with a big stone to smoke.

It's 10:30 a.m., and it's going to be my first hit of the day. I've been craving all morning, since I got up about 7:30. I should have been to work hours ago, but I needed to wait until I could get some stone and get straight before I could face the day. My hands are shaking with anticipation as I take the small glass cutting board I always carry under the seat of my car and place it on my lap, grab the tiny plastic bag out of my shirt pocket, and cut off the knot at the end of the bag with my blade. Out plops the stone onto the glass. It's about one quarter inch in diameter, a yellowish-white soft rock of dope that my dealer has told me is the "best shit" to come into town in a long time.

Trembling and anxious, working hard to control my fingers, I slice off a small portion of the stone. I take the (still large) remaining rock and place it into a small piece of tin foil, wrap it up neatly, and tuck it into a deep corner of my pants pocket. *Lots left*, I think to myself, as I am chopping and working the crack into a coarse powder on the cutting board. Once satisfied that it's sufficiently broken down and scraped into a neat little pile, I take my heater, position the char-loaded end directly over it, and suck the substance up into the end of the stem. With my loaded heater held upright (so as to not spill any), I reach for my favorite lighter, the one with the most firepower, strike it lit, and expertly burn on the dope to the char. Not enough fire to light the stuff, just enough to melt it a little, so it is a solid that won't slop out when I take a real hit. The stinky sweet fragrance, now permeating the inside of the car, overwhelms me with greed for gratification.

I look at the prepped stem, loaded with crack cocaine. *It's a Mother Load*, I think to myself: *Easily four good hits, and a couple of "push hits" after that!* Eyeballing the parking lot one more time and satisfied that no one is watching me, I duck down below the dashboard, strike up the lighter, hold the flame up to the loaded end of the heater, and begin firing up the stone. As soon as I hear that crackling noise, I lower the flame, and heat the end of the stem perimeter, as I pull the smoke into my lungs. My girlfriend taught me to do this part just right; otherwise, the dope burns up in one hit. If you fire it correctly and then work it, pulling it with the heat, so the stone melts into the char as you inhale, you'll get multiple hits out of the same load.

Once my lungs are full to the point of near explosion, I drop the lighter, fall back in my seat, and hold the smoke in as long as I can. Then, I slowly exhale through my nostrils. Instantly, a wave of euphoria and ecstasy envelops me. I am high, so high, so happy and carefree. I feel confident, strong, like Superman! I savor the high for a few moments, turn on the radio, and tune in a favorite jam. Then, as the high fades (it only takes a few minutes with crack), I pull the heater back out and look at it. I can see the melted cocaine, saturated throughout the char, all there, waiting for my pleasure. I take my pusher and move the loaded char up to the very end of the stem.

Properly primed for, the second hit is usually the best one; the strongest and most potent one, and this toke is no disappointment. The smoke comes thick, dense and plentiful, and as my lungs get filled to capacity, I slam back in my seat and savor the rush, eventually and gradually, ejecting a warm bluish gray saccharine vapor. My tongue and gums go numb as I feel my head blowing up. Now I'm wide as a football field, high as a freaking kite. I wait a couple minutes and then take the third hit. Satisfied for now and telling myself I'll save the last hit and the possible push hits for a little bit later, I turn on the car ignition and pull off into traffic, blasted out of my mind on crack.

****

You may be thinking I'm a typical nineteen-year-old stupid and confused ghetto kid with no education, from a broken home, with an abusive, alcoholic, absentee father, but I'm not. I'm a middle-aged, professional, Caucasian family man, with three wonderful, well-adjusted, fully-grown children and six grandchildren. Not long ago, I was still living happily with my wife of nearly 30 years, had the respect of my son and daughters, and was considered a good role model who could be counted on for guidance and counseling in the areas of morals, ethics and spirituality. I was an ordained Buddhist lay-minister, who did volunteer work at the state prison, teaching meditation classes to inmates seeking spiritual growth and direction. As a child, I had wonderful parents and a stable, loving, family life, with a Christian minister for a father. Neither of my parents, nor anyone in my extended family that I knew, had any bad habits or substance abuse problems. I went to college and built a successful business. Just a few short years ago, I was teaching a skilled trades class to recovering addicts and ex-convicts, helping them with their progress and rehabilitation, assisting them in finding employment and a successful return to society as productive citizens!

So *what happened to me?*

I romanced the stone ….

CHAPTER TWO:

THERE ONCE WAS A HAPPY HIPPIE

I'm a "Baby-Boomer." I'm part of the largest swell of off-spring ever seen in U.S.A. history, the generation of kids born to the men and women who celebrated the victory of World War II. For most, it was a gloriously ideal and happy time, the 1950s. The world had just been rid of the most terrifying tyrant in modern history, Adolf Hitler. The United States had emerged from the war as the world's foremost respected super-power. New technologies were abundant, bringing more comfort and luxuries to the average middle-class person than ever before. With plentiful and lucrative employment opportunities, due to the rapid growth of industry, middle-income Americans swelled into the largest class of the country. My parents' generation built bigger homes, began to own more vehicles, had more money to save and invest in their retirements, took more vacations, and lived larger than any previous generation in our country's history.

There *were* beginning to be troublesome signals coming from the Soviets and their stated plans for world dominance. Racism and the inequality of men and women were still un-dealt-with issues that would give rise to turbulence in the '60s. However, for a good decade and a half after the war ended, for the majority of young adults in America and their well-defined nuclear families, the world seemed a warm, cozy, wonderful place in which to raise children and look forward to a safe, secure and promising future together. So they mated like no generation had ever before, and no generation since has even come *close* to the amount of procreation-driven sexual activity that went on in the bedrooms of America during that time.

Those poor unwitting, happy, sexually active and comfortable folks had no *idea* what a litter of troublemakers they were giving birth to! All their ideals, religious and moral convictions, sociological and familial patterns, and political beliefs were about to be summarily rejected by a mammoth generation of ungrateful and disillusioned youngsters, who grew up to become historically famous for producing the Women's Rights movement, the Gay Rights movement, the Black Panthers and the Black Pride movement, and, of course, the most audacious and abundant group of social misfits ever to fly in the face of their parents, the Hippies!

Ah, yes, the Hippie Generation: the "counter-drug-culture." We were going to change the world with "sex, drugs, and rock and roll." The "Love Generation," The "Flower Children": We rejected nearly every belief held dear by our parents. And although we disdained them for being complacent, duped conformists in a Big Brother police state fraught with hypocrisy and corruption, we soon became conformists ourselves, only with a new set of "liberal" beliefs that were to be adhered to if one was to be accepted. A short list of Hippie-isms follows:

- The government was corrupt beyond repair and should be either overthrown and replaced with anarchy (as the Yippies, our militant branch, believed) or (at the very least) not participated in.
- No one over the age of 30 was to be trusted. They were all "in on it"; the preservation of a "Big Brother" society that kept us all in the societal corral, like a herd of cattle or sheep.
- It was best to simply "drop out": drop out of school (you were just being brainwashed), drop out of society, and drop out of "the establishment" that held us in

constraining fetters.

- Drugs, especially mind-expanding substances, marijuana, LSD, peyote, psilocybin, etc., were *good!* They opened your awareness and "The Doors of Perception" to the universal truths and communion with God.
- Casual sex with multiple partners was acceptable and encouraged. The nuclear family and the idea that one should pick out and mate one person of the opposite sex for life was largely rejected. If it worked for you, cool. But for most of us, loving someone had nothing to do with sexual "faithfulness." If you couldn't be with the one you loved, honey, you simply loved the one you were with.
- Rock and Roll was the vehicle of the message, and it was *better* than music.
- Jesus was beautiful, but contemporary Christianity and the organized church equaled a pathetic, empty, insidious, even *evil* misrepresentation of what He had really taught. We read His words such as, "turn the other cheek" and "love thine enemies," and the Jesus teachings gave rise to one of the hallmark Hippie mottos:
- *"Make Love, not War"*

So, **"Tune In"** (to the vibes, the Universal Love, the unifying "oneness" of all beings), **"Turn On"** (to drugs, especially marijuana and LSD), and "**Drop Out"** (of society) became the three main components of the Hippie Faith, sort of the Three Commandments, if you will. And I, like so many others, did just that. Within two years, I went from being a church-going, virgin choirboy, to a weed-smoking, acid-dropping, womanizing rock & roll player. I felt good about myself and my way of life. I was a happy hippie, getting high, playing music for a living, exploring the strange and brave new world.

Using drugs for fun and recreation was a part of our everyday way of life. There was nothing wrong with it, we believed, and in fact we considered it *necessary* to take at least a few acid trips to get "un-brainwashed" and *"see through all the bullshit, man."*

For some considerable length of time, this lifestyle worked for me. I had all kinds of immediate gratification, and I had a sense of purpose that I was contributing toward a better and more liberated future world to live in. Eventually, however, after several years of finding happiness through the use of drugs, powerful music, and frequent casual sexual encounters, I began to feel emptiness inside.

I started thinking that there had to be more to life than this. For every artificial (drug-induced) high, there followed a low, a state of depression. I started looking at couples who were obviously in love, and I began sort of envying the real passion and joy they seemed to share.

One day in my early 20's, I was on the road in Canada, traveling with the band. I was in my hotel room and had taken a tab of Purple Haze. Just as I was lifting off with the high, I happened to notice a Bible lying on top of the TV. Opening it up, I began reading from the New Testament.

The red words (the quoted words of Jesus) were suddenly so vivid, and their meaning so clear to me. I couldn't believe it. *What He is saying is so true. How could I have ever doubted the veracity of this God-Man?* I thought. Spinning through one hallucinogenic spiritual experience after another, I spent the entire trip (three or four hours) reading the scriptures, and it was a life-altering experience. Spirituality became the focal point of my desire and attention from that day on.

I began devouring books on all the world religions, dozens and dozens of them. In addition to the Bible, I read several of the ancient Upanishads; the Koran; the Baghavad Gita; the Dhammapada and some of the Buddhist Sutras; ancient Christian texts, such as The Gospel According to Thomas, the Gnostic Gospels, the Nag Hammadi Library and treatises on the Dead Sea Scrolls; and the works of contemporary spiritual leaders like Ram Dass, Thomas Merton, Baghwan Shree Rajneesh, Allan Watts and others. It seemed obvious to me that all the historical spiritual leaders, upon whose ministries were founded the various great world religions, were basically teaching the same quintessential truths: Krishna, Buddha, Jesus, Mohammed, were all essentially representatives of the same beacon of truth and light, leading mankind to the threshold of enlightenment.

I tried joining the Hippie "Jesus Freak" movement but found the return to organized Christian churches still too sterile and repulsive, and our young radical constituency was roundly met with rejection from the "established" congregation, for our appearance and overly jubilant singing, dancing, etc., during the meetings. After trying services from several other world religions, I just sort of gave up on finding a church/mosque/temple that I could be comfortable in.

Then, one day I was browsing through a used bookstore, and came upon a book simply entitled "Zen Meditation." I don't even remember the author's name. In it was a straightforward explanation of Zen practice, and "practice" was the key word. Here was a religion for people who don't like religion. It was not about reading scriptures, going to church, giving testimony, making a public display of your faith, and so on. It was about your personal meditation practice, your own efforts at getting to the bottom of who, and what, you are, and that being Buddha. We are all endowed with Buddha Nature, it taught, and all beings are Buddha, whether they have awakened (become enlightened) to that yet or not. At last, I had found a "non-religion" that laid out a path for spiritual growth, devoid of meaningless scripture memorizations and church meetings.

To make a long (and divergent) story short, I took up

the path of Zen Buddhism, found (and studied under) a certified Korean Zen Master for four years, and became an ordained Buddhist Lay-Minister in my early 30's. By this time I was married with three children and growing a successful business. I was a well-adjusted man, firmly grounded on a spiritual path, and although no longer the happy hippie, I was comfortable with myself and my way of life. I liked the man I saw in the mirror and went to bed each night feeling good about myself.

However, the use of drugs and mood-altering substances, albeit drastically reduced in frequency and quantity from my earlier wilder years, still remained part of my life. Nothing to worry about, of course; a couple of beers in the evening, just to "un-stress" after a hard and productive day's work, and far less frequently a few tokes off a marijuana cigarette with my old hippie friends. I considered myself a controlled and temperate drinker, and a sensible (recreational use only) marijuana smoker. The idea of "Just Say No" as a blanket statement regarding any and all drug use was ridiculous to me. After all, it was an LSD trip that had awakened me to the need for pursuit of spiritual matters. Marijuana and alcohol had always been with me in my adult life, and I had turned out all right, so what was the big fuss about?

CHAPTER THREE:

JUST SAY NO -- ARE YOU KIDDING ME?

DISCLAIMER: the author does not necessarily hold all the views, attitudes and opinions contained in this chapter today. They are intended (and should be considered by the reader) as primarily background material that will help lead into some meaningful conclusions in the final chapters of this book.

When our First Lady at the time, Nancy Reagan, came out with her "Just Say No" to drugs slogan and campaign in the eighties, I and many other (now middle-class) ex-hippies just laughed and scoffed at the entire message. Highly addictive narcotics, like heroin, opium and cocaine, had always been on my no-no list, but the idea of lumping marijuana and hallucinogens in with that group of drugs was absurd to me.

I was amazed at how successfully this attitude swept over the country. I watched and listened in disbelief, as I saw and heard my generation, most of which (better than 60 percent) [1] had smoked marijuana as teenagers and young adults, but now "conscientious" and "straight" members of the society they once derailed, jump onto the "Just Say No" bandwagon. Now married and raising children, they felt they needed to "set the right example" for the younger generation and the good of their kids.

Oh, my Lord, you people are going to make me throw up, I thought. It was as though an entire generation had suffered a convenient memory loss over what they had been like as young people. Suddenly, it was immoral, and unhealthy, to do any kinds of drugs. The blatant irony of it, the absolute unabashed hypocrisy exhibited by the grown-up flower children, was totally disgusting to me.

We had not only failed in our attempts to change the world, we had now become very much like our parents in terms of so-called morality. And to make matters worse, we did not have innocence or naiveté to fall back on as an excuse!

Let's have a little fun poking at the "Just Say No" philosophy and the "reformed" Boomers who bought into it and propagate it to this day. If you are going to "just say no" to drugs because: (A) they are harmful to your body and mind, and/or (B) it is illegal to use them, then doesn't it also follow that:

- Alcohol, the most abused and harmful drug in our society, should be said "no" to. Should not alcohol consumption be illegal? Shouldn't we go back to prohibition? How many parents are telling their kids to "just say no" while sipping on an adult beverage?
- The U.S. population holds the distinction of being the most overweight society in the world, with the highest percentage of obesity, and our percentage of obese children has been steadily increasing over the past several decades. How many fat parents, with high blood pressure and rising cholesterol counts, have told their offspring to "just say no" to drugs, all the while teaching them (by example) how to eat themselves into poor health and an early death? Shouldn't there be a legal height-to-weight ratio limit, and anyone who exceeds it be thrown in jail for a 30-day fast, followed with a two-year forced and supervised probationary diet? Grocery stores selling to food abusers should be fined on the first offense and have their licenses to sell food revoked on the second offense,

right?

- The Baby Boomers are now getting old and developing the normal attendant physical pains that come with aging. The result in terms of drug usage? Narcotics-based painkillers (like Oxycontin, Ultram, Valium and Vicadin) are now becoming among the most-abused drugs in our country. You can even buy them over the Internet without a doctor's prescription. TV ads advise us to "tell your doctor you want "such and such" … at this point hasn't your doctor now become your *dealer?* If we are telling our kids to not take any drugs, shouldn't we be able to take the pain and "just say no" to these addictive drugs? Yes, yes, of course we should, and all these drugs should be illegal, and their users should be incarcerated.
- Coffee, tea, Coca-Cola and most soft drinks, including many of the now popular "energy drinks," contain caffeine, which is an addictive drug. They should just be said "no" to. Caffeine should be illegal, and its use at least a misdemeanor, punishable by up to 90 days in the pen and a $500 fine. Plea bargains of no less than six months' probation and community service would help our youth understand the importance of "just saying no" to the Devil's Drinks.
- Although cigarette smoking is now banned in all U.S. public buildings, nearly all retail stores, restaurants, offices and professional buildings, and even *bars* in some cities, many Americans continue to smoke. The addictive qualities of nicotine, and the physical dangers of using tobacco, are probably the most documented and proven of all the drugs today. But I'll bet there are plenty of children being instructed to "just say no" while inhaling secondhand smoke in their homes. This should be a felony; "intent to do bodily harm," with a minimum 10-year prison sentence, and our schools should encourage children to report their smoking parents to the police.
- How many children have been given the "just say no"

talk by a parent who is driving the car 5-10 miles per hour (or more) over the legal speed limit? I say, "Arrest that man or woman, flog him or her, put the children in foster care homes, and send the criminals off to jail!"

I could go on and on, and get even more outrageously sarcastic and cynical, but I think you get the picture by now. And of course, I know that another doesn't right one wrong. If you already have bad habits, and are obviously addiction-prone, even dabbling with dangerously addictive narcotics is just asking for serious trouble. But, good grief, the sheer magnitude of hypocrisy exhibited by my generation with regard to any and all drug usage was nothing less than an embarrassment to me.

When President Bill Clinton was confronted publicly with the report that some of his fraternity brothers in college had told journalist sources that the President used to smoke marijuana at frat parties they attended, he had the *audacity* to say that he had "never inhaled!" As adults, we all have learned how to "doublethink" (a la Orwell's "1984") so even though we can think to ourselves that this is an untruth, we allow it to stand as the truth. But what about the message we are sending our not yet jaded, disillusioned, or brainwashed children? Can he, and all of us in our generation, consider our children *that* stupid? Do we guess that we can cover up our past, and lie in the face of our kids, and tell them to "do as we say, and not as we have done," all the while continuing to abuse our bodies and minds with "legal" drugs and bad habits? Give me a living break!

What happened to the virtue of temperance? Where's the Yin-Yang wisdom? Have we all gone mad in this country?

It is human nature to want what is forbidden. Remember the Biblical story of Adam and Eve in the Garden of Eden? All the abundance of foods at their disposal to eat of as they pleased, without having to do any labor, and what do they wind up cherishing as their most desired fruit? The forbidden fruit of the Tree of Knowledge, of course. What we're told we cannot have becomes the object of our strongest desire.

Here in the United States of Hypocrisy, we tell our children to not drink alcohol, to not do any drugs, and to not smoke tobacco. Of course many adults do some or all of these things, but for some obscure reason, we decide that these "adult" indulgences should be reserved for anyone who has attained a certain arbitrary age. We vote on what that age should be from time to time, but for the most part it is 18 for smoking, 21 for drinking, and *never* for "illegal" drugs. Protecting our children, right? Making sure they live healthy lives, right?

Wrong.

It wasn't until the 1920s that narcotics were made illegal. Until that time, the general consensus was that laws should not be used to regulate personal behavior. In fact, the Bayer Company introduced "heroin" as a brand name, for a seemingly very useful respiratory ailment drug in 1898. Were there narcotics addicts back then? Of course there were. But creating laws against their use, making them now "forbidden fruits," scarcely got rid of the problem; it rather exacerbated it. Now we had addicts *and* occasional users, who were all now *criminals*, and a whole global syndicate of criminal suppliers, distributors and pushers to fuel the illicit industry.[2]

Has the problem gotten any better? Have narcotics addiction levels in our society decreased from the 1920s to the present? Have we seen a decrease in crime rates (especially drug-abuse-related crime) since then? You answer that one.

In Switzerland, the legal drinking age is 14. Common sense would tell us that they must have a higher rate of alcoholics over there than we do, right? Wrong again, folks. They have less of a problem. From 1961 to 2001, there was no gain in percentage of alcohol users among their overall population, and their percentage of binge drinkers among young adults was lower (25 percent among males and 6 percent among females) [3] than ours (38.5 percent overall). [4] Why? Because of the "Forbidden Fruit" syndrome, of course!

In France, nudity is not considered to be such a monumental moral taboo as it is here in the United Puritans of America. Therefore, it would follow that they must have a higher rate of sexual assaults over there, right? Wrong once more; just the opposite is true: They have fewer sex crimes there (2 percent of adult women reporting sexual assault) [5] than we do here (7.7 percent of adult women sexually assaulted). [6]

Consider third world countries in temperate climates, where it is the tradition and custom for women to go about naked from the waist up. Do those men lose their senses and commit sexual crimes against their women because of such a sight? Of course not; they are accustomed to it.

Yet here in the United States of False-Righteousness, where nudity is by and large illegal and considered by the vast majority to be immoral, the sight of one of Janet Jackson's breasts "accidentally" exposed on prime-time TV is cause for national media headline coverage, and the primary subject of tabloid prattle and talk show agendas, for months! Illegal, seedy, pimp-delivered street prostitution; strip bars; pornographic literature, movies, and brazen TV shows, not to mention the endless pop-up sexually explicit and graphic websites cumming all over our monitors, are how we American men get our "forbidden fruit" served up to us. And we have a huge appetite for it, subsidizing a multi-billion dollar industry, with our insatiable cravings for exactly that which we are not supposed to want or have. Our social ethics, religious morals, and governmental laws tell us we cannot have it, yet our entrepreneurial-driven marketplace dangles it in front of our noses every waking moment of our lives.

Our society is one of fundamental contradictions. We want to be free and feel happy. The use of drugs and alcohol can produce a temporary (yet false) sense of both. We produce these things, offer them up enticingly for consumption, and then turn around and legislate and warn against the use of them. Our entertainment industry markets infidelity and libido to us as though it is the ultimate pleasure in life and makes idols out of our movie stars and their glamorous "anything goes" sex lives. We believe in truth, honesty, justice and integrity. But we live in a society where our political leaders are consistently revealed as having lied to us, our priests (certainly not all, but enough to cause disbelief and alarm) are discovered to be pedophiles, our judicial system has dual standards for the rich and the poor, and for our young people, finding a role model with enough true integrity to emulate is like trying to find a snowball in Hell.

So, tell me, Mrs. Reagan; please, please, Nancy … just what *exactly* on God's green earth should we be saying "no" to? Drugs and alcohol? You're telling me *that's* the real problem here? I beg to differ, Madame. Rather, we should be saying "no" to some very real, fundamental and dangerous problems with our society and our way of creating and dealing with our reality in daily life. Drugs and alcohol, in and of themselves, are not the problem. It is our desire and need to use them to excess that is the real issue that needs to be addressed. Your "just say no" campaign is a perfunctory and pathetic effort to place a non-stick Band-Aid on a cancerous tumor and then pronounce the patient "cured."

CHAPTER FOUR

GROWING UP AND GETTING STRAIGHT

By the mid-1980s, it was obvious to me that the Hippies had failed in any way to make positive, lasting changes in our society. Spiritualism and idealism gave way (and turned in) to good old-fashioned American consumerism, but now on steroids. By then, the Hippies had evolved into the awful antithesis of everything they had once stood for: the selfish, materialistic, greedy Yuppies. They were the largest group of ambitious and officious capitalists to ever hit Wall Street, and the stock market ballooned with inflated growth. Buying and selling real estate with "creative" deals, corporate mega-mergers, and hostile take-overs became the game, and lots of Boomers got rich. Bigger homes, fancier cars, all the latest entertainment gadgetry, and lavish lifestyles, it was the new high: the STUFF of life! One bumper sticker I read said it all: "Whoever dies with the most toys wins!"

Oh, sure, the Black Pride movement had gotten a few "token Blacks" into positions of authority. There were "African-Americans" starring in movies and TV shows, the occasional "colored" face on the professional pitcher's mound and shining out through the quarterback's helmet, and Negroes no longer had to sit in the back of the bus. But the KKK was still alive and kicking, the Neo-Nazis and the White Pride movement was growing, Martin Luther King Jr. had been shot to death, and the ghettos were still there, ugly as sin and full of drugs and crime. The Gay Liberation movement had Elton John singing the rich man's blues during same-sex marriages, and the Women's Rights movement was growing balls larger than church bells. But the

Hippies … they were gone, replaced by their reprehensible metamorphoses, the sexy, greedy, self-centered Yuppies.

Now the Yuppies had rebelled against everything their parents had stood for as young Hippies, and as a consequence, they learned very little about good parenting. And the net result of the "sexy-'70s"-casual-sex-free-love era was lots and lots of little bastards running around, with scarcely anyone home who knew how to raise them. Parenting skills had become a lost art, and the ability to keep marriage vows had atrophied in our society to the point where divorce rates were skyrocketing and single parenting became normal. Pursuit of pleasure, personal success, and happiness was more important than integrity and faithfulness. And if "getting all I can get out of life for myself" conflicted with being there for the spouse and/or the children, well, they'd just have to make do, you only live once, and by God, I'm going to be all that I can be. That was the attitude, and even the magazine shelves began reflecting it, offering popular new publications with titles like "Self" and "All You."

In the late '80s, I happened just by chance, to run into Sandy, one of my old hippie buddies. "Handy Sandy" we used to call him, because he could fix anything; and as the most gifted pothead among us in that regard, also with a good ear for music, he had been the head roadie and sound engineer for our rock & roll band back in the'70s. Back then, he was a well-built, muscular guy, tall, with shoulder-length brown hair, mischievous blue eyes twinkling in concert with an engaging smile, and he possessed a marvelous penchant for cracking hilarious off-color jokes. I was overjoyed to meet up with him, of course, but now he was quite different. He had gained a lot of weight, lost some hair, I could swear there was a gray film over his once-bright blue eyes, and the old ever-present smile had been replaced with a rather somber and burdensome countenance. He certainly didn't look like he was having any fun. At least, nothing like the rowdy fun we used to have.

We used to drop acid and smoke weed together, share sex with groupies, drink volumes of beer, and all the rest that goes with that lifestyle, but when I began to reminisce about the "good old days," he informed me that he would prefer not to talk about those things anymore. He explained that he had since married, was raising kids, and was now going "the Way of the Lord." He felt he had to become a religious teetotaler in order to set the right example for his children.

He was now a confirmed "just say no" kind of guy, with typical grownup boomer black-and-white thinking. The church had been right all along, the President was to be respected, our wars were all justified, and Mom's apple pie was better after dinner than a couple of cold ones.

I myself had to admit that I was now a grownup, no longer the idealistic little Peter Pan Pothead of yore, but I was bound and determined that I would not yield to this complete mental reversal and disavowing of everything I had once stood for. I knew that drug-induced spiritual experiences were not the real thing, so I had replaced hallucinogens with Zen meditation. I knew excessive pot smoking tended to make one lazy, so I had reduced the use of it drastically, in order to focus clearly on building my business. I remembered how I had rebelled at the amount of stifling rules and religious constraints my parents had imposed on me, so I set about raising my children with a more freewheeling and organic approach to ethical, moral and spiritual guidance.

As I witnessed the majority of my generation acquiesce to the system, buy into the politics, yield to consumer-driven materialism, return to church on Sundays, and rewire their brains to accept "doublethink" truths as reality, I staunchly held on to my maverick posture as an outsider, an independent thinker and rebel at heart, even though I knew the war had been lost. Ex-hippies were becoming C.E.O.'s of major corporations, politicians, and capitalists with (in many cases) less-than-ethical standards. It was not how you played the game but whether or not you won; that was all that mattered.

I was growing a small business of my own during the ‘80s, and I promised myself that it would be a fair and honest enterprise, one that gave good service and product, for a reasonable and fair price. I treated capitalism as a necessary, but dangerous and addictive drug, one that had to be used wisely and cautiously, less one become addicted to it and let it turn into the sole desire of the soul: making money for the love of money. I knew that money was not the root of all evil, but the *love* of money *was* a false god that my generation had by and large come to worship.

So I continued into the ‘90s on the road less traveled, refusing to give in to the brainwashing I felt my boomer generation had submitted itself to. I was happily married, had three wonderful children, was growing a successful business, and had a spiritual path that resonated well with me and kept me feeling centered and good about life. I often thought back fondly of the good old days when hippies roamed the earth, and I felt a sense of failure and loss now that the inevitable had happened so slowly and inexorably.

The Hippies had grown up and gotten straight in the process, and the Yuppies now ruled the planet.

CHAPTER FIVE

THE UNHAPPY YUPPIE

Now that the idealistic but unrealistic and naïve Hippies had fully converted into their grownup counterparts, the Yuppies, we entered the nonsensical '90s. Fraught with double standards, double-thinking and hypocrisy, here we had a majority class of people who had rejected and dispensed with the ways of their parents, spent their youthful years conforming to a "brave new world" philosophy, and finally settled back into the very society they initially dropped out of. The "Hippie-isms" that were held in the mid-'60s to late-'70s as truths gave way to the "new" beliefs and mannerisms of the Yuppies:

Hippies	Yuppies
- No one over the age of 30 is to be trusted	- No one under the age of 30 has any idea what's really going on, and the old folks (over 60) are soon dying off, nothing to worry about.
- Drugs are good for you, especially LSD.	- Officially, All illegal drugs are bad for you, especially for the kids. Unofficially, doing lines of cocaine at upscale Yuppie parties is OK. But be discreet, and don't let the children know.

-We should all "drop out" of the system.	-We should all work within the system.
- We are all one big family, a brotherhood of man.	-I'm looking out for Number One.
- Go barefoot, wear sandals, or wear "Earth Shoes."	- Wear expensive Italian leathers.
-Jesus is cool.	-Church is boring, and even though I find no real meaning there, it's important to go to church for the children's sake.
-Rock and Roll is the message and voice of our generation, and it is better than the. music of our parents.	-Punk rock is just noise, and rap music sucks. How can this young generation listen to that crap?
- The government is corrupt.	-The government can do whatever it wants, as long as it allows me to make money.
-Free love and casual sex is OK.	-Love comes with a price, and casual sex can kill you. Get married, or practice "safe sex," or "just say no."
-Make love, not war	-War is good if it serves our country's best interests. If innocent lives are being killed, just don't make me think about it.
-Tune in, Turn on, and Drop out.	- Tune into the System, Turn on your TV, and Buy as much stuff as you can.

What a miserable lot we were, drinking our martinis, groveling in our wealth and accumulations, popping our legal pills, and attempting to raise a "generation X" of "slackards," without a clue as to why they were such a misbehaving, lazy bunch, (due to our convenient memory loss with regard to how *we* were at their age). Brain-dead and submissive, devoid of any true spiritual grounding, and without a leg to stand on except the prosthetic of hypocrisy, we muddled our way through the '90s as best we could. Failures as parents, failures as spouses, failures as governmental reformists, failures as idealists, failures as people of integrity in the marketplace, failures as spiritualists, failures, failures, failures, that's what we were.

Now that's a broad generalization, mind you, and I do apologize to those readers who are, and/or know of, the wonderful exceptions to the rule. Many ex-hippies and others of my generation went on to become good, solid people; people of integrity, true spiritualists, just leaders, well-adjusted and fair business people, and family members, etc. We didn't *all* turn out that bad. It was the 98 out of 100 who gave the other two such a bad reputation (Joking ... *I'm joking!)*. Still and all, as a generation that once considered itself to be a bastion of personal, political and spiritual freedoms, we knew in our hearts that nothing much had changed at all.

As the new millennium was ushered in, the boomer generation was a disillusioned lot, attempting to raise a generation of young adults who were even more disillusioned. And the meaningless "just say no" campaign was an exercise in futility, as evidenced by the alarming *increase* in numbers of *both* generations that were numbing their physical, emotional, psychological and spiritual pain with self-medications.

Turn of the century surveys on national drug abuse conducted in 2000 and 2001 by the Substance Abuse and Mental Health Services Administration (SAMHSA) reported that:

- Among 20 year olds, 38.5 percent were "binge" drinkers, and 14.2 percent "heavy" drinkers.
- Alcohol usage among the "under-age" youth was starting at about age 12 (2.4 percent) and increasing every year up to the age of 20, at 55.6 percent.
- In 2000, among youths between 12 and 17 years of age, 9.7 were illegal drug users. That number increased the next year to 10.8 percent.
- During the same period, illegal drug use among young adults between 18 and 25 years of age went from 15.9 to 18.9 percent.
- Admitted crack users among 18 to 25 year olds was at 3.4 percent and rose to 4.5 percent among those between 26 and 34; 5.1 percent between 35 and 49, and even some of the aging boomers (over 50) had tried the stuff (.5 percent).
- 1.4 percent of the population admitted to the use of heroin.
- 7.2 percent of the population, of all ages, 12 through 50 & older, had used stimulants, 3 percent had been sedative users, and 6.2 percent had used tranquilizers.
- The majority of boomers (55 percent of those 50 or older) were using alcohol 100 days or more during the year.
- Oddly enough, *the use of pain relievers was highest among the youth*, ages 18 to 25, at 1.2 percent. Hmm … I wonder *what kind of pain they are relieving?*
- And the old standby, marijuana? 40 percent of the population admitted to the use of marijuana at one time or another; 20 percent of 12 to 17 year olds, increasing to an average of around 50 percent for all those between 18 and 49.
- ***Of those over the age of 50, only 18 percent admitted to <u>ever</u> using marijuana!***

Liars, liars, liars! I suspect that *all* the numbers reported on these types of surveys are skewed and faulted by the boomers' inability to tell the truth, what with their convenient memory loss and the rapidly growing Alzheimer's Disease epidemic. I mean, if the President of the United Sates can deny, in front of the national media, that he ever smoked pot *with eyewitnesses to the contrary*, who are *they* to tell the truth and disillusion their children about what angels they were in *their* youth?

The same report referred to above shows that in 2001, there were 5 million Americans who were classified as "in need of treatment" for substance abuse but not receiving it. Of those, only 377,000 (7.5 percent) *were willing to admit that they needed help*!

Denial, boomers, denial; it's those little white lies that haunt you, and taunt you. Your children are following your example, and the sins of the fathers are being visited upon the sons.

I have painted a rather dismal portrait of the '90s, and again, in a lot of ways, perhaps mostly with my use of generalizations, I have been unfair to many good people who stand for and represent truth, honesty, integrity, etc. All is not lost, but then not much has been gained, either. My life through most of the '90s was a good one, building my business, happily married, and raising my children. By the end of the decade, however, events and situations would take a turn for the worse, and my life would go off in a direction I had never thought possible for someone like me. Things were going to get very ugly.

CHAPTER SIX

THE GOOD GUY TURNS BAD AND GETS UGLY

By the mid-1990s, my wife and I had built a rather successful small business and were enjoying a fairly comfortable lifestyle. You know, the six-figure income, a nice house to live in, driving new cars, lots of credit cards, fun vacations, dining out at fancy restaurants, attending the theater, going to concerts, clubbing at night, buying all the latest in computer and entertainment gadgetry; it made life seem good and easy. But there was one problem that was creeping up on me from behind that I was not conscious of. I had gotten lazy.

Not lazy with regard to work and career, I was still a driven and motivated entrepreneur, determined to be more and more successful in the business world; no, I had gotten lazy with regard to matters of the heart and soul. I was so wrapped up in the pursuit of better lifestyle, I had lost focus on what was happening to me as a person. I was less communicative with and affectionate toward my wife. I spent less and less time with my kids. I rarely communicated with my parents, brothers and extended family.

I was feeling like I could have anything I wanted, that the world had to offer. It was a true "Yuppie-think" mentality. My mind started indulging in fantasies about having a little extra sex "on the side." Hey, what's the harm, lots of men going through their "mid-life-crisis" have an occasional tryst with a younger woman, right? I stopped practicing my Zen meditation, no time for that, and no money in it. I was working so hard, six days a week, that I felt I needed at least one day to relax completely, so I stopped my volunteer work at the state prison, teaching meditation to the inmates. I rarely read books anymore, preferring to watch TV and drink alcoholic beverages in the evening, to "unwind."

My addiction to "the good life" was insidious. It fooled me, and crept up on me, like a magician creating a masterful illusion. And I soon came to find out that my wonderfully materialistic life was just that: an illusion.

Like many greedy, self-centered people of my generation, I had fallen prey to the credit game. Yes, my income was around $100,000 per year, which was *plenty* of money at the time if managed wisely, but I was spending around *$110,000* per year, with the careless and uncontrolled use of credit cards. As the business grew and grew in gross revenues, I elevated my lifestyle higher and higher, not paying heed to the sound business principle of capitalizing the company with profits before taking the money home. I was playing a leapfrog money game, spending money before it was earned, and making up for it by earning more and more each year, only to again outspend the earnings. Although I had the outward *appearance* of success, I had no money saved in the bank; no significant equity in my home or possessions, and was by 1996 a full-blown "cash-flow addict" with more than $30,000 of credit card debt. Then I got busted.

To abbreviate a depressing story, within two years the company went broke due to a tailspin of downward-spiraling cash flow, brought about by some frivolous and hostile litigation. One year later, I had to file for Chapter 7 bankruptcy in order to be able to keep my home and at least one vehicle. With all my toys taken away, no money, and no income, I was broke and broken down.

I was broke financially, mentally, emotionally and spiritually. My wife and I drifted further and further apart. The stress of economic reversal seemed to drive a wedge between our already separated hearts. We both were drinking heavily in the evenings, and often times the liquor would loosen us up to the point where we would openly express ourselves, and more often than not, it would turn into an argument, sometimes heated and even vicious.

Fortunately, the children were mostly grown by now and out of the house. We had never put on this kind of selfish and stupid display of lack of love, maturity and wisdom in front of them as they were growing up. Oh, yes, of course, we had had our domestic quarrels, as most married and parenting couples do, but nothing like this. Even though grown, our children lived nearby and saw us often enough to recognize that there were some real problems with our marriage, and they all expressed their concern for us and the amount of alcohol we were drinking.

And the situation just kept getting worse. For a short time after the demise of our company, we managed to squeeze by with my wife working at a low-paying job and me taking a teaching position in a trade school in a nearby city. Gone were the perks and the fun things, and the bills were larger than our checks, but we somehow got along for a while although we continued to drift farther and farther apart. We became just roommates and not very compatible ones at that.

After about a year and a half, I lost my job due to a school funding cut and plunged full time into the world of multi-level marketing. I really thought I had found the answer with this venture. I was going to the meetings, hearing the incredible success stories of those who had amassed fortunes and now lived carefree and lavish lifestyles, with residual incomes that would bring wealth to them and their descendents for generations to come. I became one of the most sought after speakers on the meeting circuit and was growing a huge "down-line."

During this time, I wanted more than anything to be

fabulously successful financially. I wanted wealth and security. I felt that if I could just get rich, everything would be fine again. All the emotional and mental pain, the depression, the sense of low self esteem and failure would dissolve, and I could buy back happiness. For a short time it seemed it was going to work. During a brief four-month period, I was making more money than ever before and was on track (at that rate of growth) to top $200,000 by the end of the year.

The past-due bills were getting paid, there was money left over to go out to dinner and treat my wife to a good time, and I was feeling like a man and getting some respect. My wife even wanted to have sex with me again, and I took this as evidence and proof that it really was “all about the money.” When I didn’t have it, I was considered to be (and felt like) a bum. When I did have it, I got respect, affection, and felt better about my life and myself.

Alas, this brief illusion of success was soon to be exposed as a castle built on sand. Quickly and surely, the organization I had built, and the cash flow income I had generated, started faltering, then sputtering and choking, and within three months had stopped producing altogether. I was broke again, a bum again, a failure again, and life at home was worse than ever. My wife was on me, every day, to give up on my naïve, lofty dreams, and get a “real job.” My kids all voiced the same opinion. For a long time, I refused to give in and in so doing give up any hope of ever being successful again. I was getting older, and since I had always made my living as a self-employed entrepreneur, I was not really qualified for any well-paid employee positions. I remained in my bullheaded, stubborn, “go for broke” mode way too long for any of my family to bear.

Eventually, I had to come to the inevitable conclusion that I was in the wrong, and they had been right all along. I gave up all hope of a bright and promising future. With hands that now ached with arthritis, I went back to doing what I had done two and a half decades earlier; I became a carpenter again, earning a modest hourly wage. Once the proud owner of a company that hired its laborers, I now had to toil in pain all day long, only to bring home less than was needed, and every night I drowned my physical and emotional pain in a bottle of vodka. I was numb, broken down, lonely and spiritually bankrupt.

And things just *kept* getting worse.

My feeble and tardy attempt at rectifying our economic mess came too little and too late. I had my only remaining vehicle repossessed. My wife and I had to sell our home to avoid its being repossessed by the bank. I tried investing what little equity we had remaining in the house in a real estate deal that went sour and lost even *that* tiny nest egg that we had hoped to parlay into a “fresh start.” That was the last straw for my wife, and one evening shortly after, she called me over to sit on the couch for a talk. She expressed to me that she wanted a separation.

We had each considered this separately at different times before, but this time it was agreed; we both wanted it now. She couldn’t stand what had become of me and our life together, and I didn’t like being around her anymore, either. We both felt we’d be better off going our separate ways, fending for ourselves for a while and, hopefully, sometime down the road, be able to rekindle our relationship, after taking some personal time off to find ourselves again. We had already co-signed a lease on a rental home, so she began saving and preparing to move out as soon as possible. I began looking for self indulgence and satisfaction elsewhere.

I determined that now was the time to gratify my fantasy of having a fresh new young lover. Hell, I didn’t care anymore. Self-esteem? Gone. Hope? Dead. Spirituality? A distant memory. Responsibility? What’s that? At this point, I was ready to have some devil-may-care adventure, some wild and crazy fun. I was about to go off on a pleasure-seeking rampage. By this time, I was drinking so heavily at night, my daughters didn't want me coming around the grandkids anymore if I was drunk. My wife had told me she had lost all respect for me, and I was starving for some (undeserved and unearned) affection. And, by God, I was going to find it and get it from somewhere and someone, even if it had to be at the basest of levels.

I decided to buy it.

I had noticed a "strip" near where I worked, where call girls hung out on the street for business. One day, I pulled over on an impulse and picked up a foxy-looking young black woman. I had long fantasized about having sex with a professional streetwalker and was in the perfect frame of mind to play out the dream. My heart thumped in awe at the thought of what I was about to do, as this female stranger slithered into my car with "How 'ya doin', baby?" drawling out of her plump, purple-painted lips. I asked what her name was. "Shuga, dahlin', everyones call me Shuga." She snickered, like maybe I was stupid enough to believe that; might as well have said "Chaka Khan."

She *was* cute, even though she had a couple of scars on her face. Way too much makeup made it difficult to determine if she was really pretty. She wore a medium-sized Afro that needed combing, was missing a couple of side teeth, and her fingernails were bit down to the quick. I guessed her to be about 30. This chick was petite and stacked, wore a black low-cut halter-top, matching skin-tight hot pants, and knee-high fake patent leather boots, had a drawer full of cheap jewelry on, and reeked of dollar-store-variety perfume. Her devious dark brown eyes were darting about constantly, and dimples that flashed in and out with the come-on looks she was giving me flanked her devilishly coy smile

We drove (at her suggestion) to a dumpy motel in the area that sold stays by the hour. I got a room for us that, although neat and freshly remade, was odiferous enough that I was grateful for her otherwise overpowering low-budget fragrance.

Now, I had had a couple of hookers for friends before, during my 20's. One I'm sure must be dead by now, unless she was able to get off her heroin addiction, but the other was putting her way through college. Both where intelligent women who were using the cards they had been dealt; one playing a day-to-day game of survival, the other playing a calculated game of chess to buy her way to freedom from the ghetto. Each of them enjoyed talking and laughing with a guy who wasn't a trick, and I was fascinated by the ability they had to use their sexuality as a money-making tool, preying on men's weaknesses to get what they wanted. They both schooled me that prostitutes have no feelings or respect, whatsoever, for their "Johns."

To hear it from them, it was like, just make sure you get all the money up front, strip down only as much as needed for the particular sex act you are being paid to perform, then grit your teeth while he does whatever he needs to do, get the guy off as quick as you can (that's where the *skill* came in), then *get him off you*. Fake an orgasm during the performance (if it's appropriate or expected), feign endearment toward the jerk, and then lie to him afterwards about how impressed you are with his masculinity and sexual prowess. Play your cards right, and you'll likely get a big tip as well as a scheduled follow-up date, thus cutting down on the amount of need to hustle on the streets, where you are always taking dangerous chances with first-time strangers. Never allow yourself to have any *real* feelings during all this play-acting; no hugging before or after the sex part, and <u>never</u> let them kiss you on the mouth.

According to my preconceptions, then, this little pickup game should have been a "pay her, bang her, and drop her off somewhere" type of experience, but this girl was an enjoyable contrast to my expectations. I could tell right away she wasn't a very seasoned pro, because she was a bit nervous about the whole thing. She was talkative and funny, and we hit it off, laughing and enjoying each other's company. When I tried kissing her, she kissed me back. She was *anything but* callous or cold during the sex, and afterwards, she wanted to cuddle and chit chat, asking me about myself, what I did for a living, where I was from, etc. She gave me her *real* name, "Letisha," and wrote down her cell phone number for me. We hung out together the rest of the afternoon. She told me she liked me and really needed a friend in her life, because she had no one she could talk to or trust, and she felt a strong connection with me, for some reason. Just recently, her fiancé had died in a fatal car crash; both her mother and best friend older sister had also died within the past three months. She lost her job as a result, because of taking so much time off, grieving, and only this past summer had turned to the streets for survival, encouraged and mentored by her other sister, who had been a prostitute for several years.

I became Letisha's Knight in Shining Armor. I expressed to her that I would like to be her friend and to have her as my lover, and that I only had two conditions: one, that she would stop prostituting herself and have sex only with me from then on; and two, that she would not use any hard drugs. She readily and thankfully agreed to my terms. She quit the streets, I helped her get by until she was able to get a job, and we struck up a relationship. Letisha heaped lavish praises upon me, called me her answer to prayer, and repeatedly expressed what a great man I was. I had found the perfect "young enough to be my daughter" pretty mistress, who constantly told me how charming, witty and handsome I was, and how much she loved me, appreciated me, and respected me. I was hearing and getting everything I needed from her. I loved her back for all this, and I derived a great sense of self-worth from the whole affair, because I felt like a real man again, able to provide and care for someone who acknowledged and thanked me for doing so. To be honest, she made me feel like some kind of hero.

Now my wife hadn't even moved out yet, so I had to start living a lie at home. I lied every day about where I was going and what I was doing. I lied to my kids, to my wife, to my employer, and I had to come up with lies about the lies I had told, in order to evade being discovered as the liar I had turned into. I hated that part of the whole farce, but I was addicted to the pleasure my deception was bringing me. I was turning into the very antithesis of everything I had once stood for and a living example of nearly everything I had always instructed my young (growing up) children *not* to be.

I shoved my conscience, integrity, morals and ethics way down deep and out of sight, in order to remain happy during the day, and drank myself into a stupor at night so I could get to sleep, careful not to look too long in the mirror and see a reflection of what I knew deep down I had become. I didn't care anymore about anything. I just did not care.

One day, about six months after we had first met, I was on a date with Letisha, and she happened to empty her purse, looking for something. I noticed a strange looking glass tube that seemed to be a pipe of some kind. When asked about it, she said she was carrying it around because she had some friends who "hit the rock," and she could get about five dollars by selling it to one of them. I quizzed her as to whether or not *she* ever "hit the rock," and she said she had once or twice in the past but didn't anymore.

Then again, a few weeks later, I noticed the same pipe in her purse. I knew something was up, that she was not leveling with me. When confronted with my asking about it, she admitted that she was an *occasional* user but assured me that it was only once and a while, and she was not strung out on the stuff. I let it go at the time, even though this was a direct violation of one of the agreed-upon conditions of our relationship.

Eventually, she began using in front of me. Not all the time and not frequently enough for me to feel alarmed that she was a hopelessly strung out crackhead. She didn't go through any visible withdrawal symptoms without it, and it seemed harmless enough that once in a while she would ask if we could stop at a certain house and pick up a small rock so she could get high. She never offered me any, and that was fine with me; I had heard and read that this was a powerfully addictive narcotic, and I was perfectly satisfied with my alcohol buzz. I was thoroughly addicted to the fun and sex we were having by now, and I was quite convinced by her overall changes in behavior, that she *was* keeping the other promise (about not turning tricks), so I didn't want to rock the love-boat, at least not for now; not unless the habit got out of hand, in my estimation.

A couple months after my quiet unspoken acceptance of her using, during a balmy spring afternoon, we were taking a walk in the park joking and talking, commenting on how beautiful the day was, sharing a chocolate milkshake. It was a magnificent, almost surreal, magical forest setting, and we were acting like a couple of high school kids. We stopped to rest on a fallen log, deep into the woods, out of sight from anyone.

After a short rest, she pulled out her pipe and loaded it up. As I watched her taking a hit of this mysterious stuff, my curiosity got the best of me. I asked her if I could try a hit. She nearly choked on her smoke, got this incredulous look on her face, and scolded me with, *"No, Hell no, Marvin, absolutely not!"* She said she really needed to quit using altogether, wished she had never started, and didn't want to see me get hooked on it. She had seen many people lose everything they had by fooling around with crack, and no way did she want that to happen to me.

But I insisted.

I told her I was a very strong-willed person, I had tried every drug that was out there at one time or another, and I could handle one little sample, just to see what it was like. After a brief argument, I overcame her resistance. She sighed and handed the pipe over to me. She showed me how to hold the glass tube, the correct amount of fire to apply, and talked me through the pull, so I would get the maximum hit out of the remaining load. In one fateful moment, I had set into motion the seed of self-destruction, and I was completely unconscious of the peril I had just put myself in.

I got a brief high and felt a sense of euphoria. We were both a bit stone silly by this time, laughing, poking and joking, and talking for a while more, then we walked back to the car and finished out our date. I thought nothing of the one hit of crack I had taken and drove home that night totally unaware that I was doomed from that day on.

About a week later, we were together again, and I asked if I could hit her pipe once more. This time she put up less resistance, and I had a couple good hits. It was an incredible high this time, although I commented that it didn't seem to last very long. A couple of days after that, we were driving through the boarded-up drug lanes of her neighborhood, and I suggested we cop some stone. She looked at me kind of sad at first, but then that sparkling smile with dimples lit up again, and she chirped out, "OK, bet."

I gave her a fifty-dollar bill and told her to score us a big enough stone to get us both really high. She scored, we shared, and we both got very high and had enough dope to keep the high going throughout the entire date. I would never have thought or admitted it at the time, but *I was already hooked on crack cocaine.*

Crack now became a central part of our dates. We smoked the rock, drank vodka, and spent our times together in a state of absolute wild and carefree oblivion, consuming more and more narcotics with each date we had. I was getting loose and reckless, sometimes so stoned I would forget just where I was, what these people I was dealing with were really all about, and what a dangerous environment I was flirting with. I was playing with fire, and although at times I would acknowledge to myself that I was walking a path of peril, part of me was reveling in the impassioned thrill of living on the edge of hazard.

One time, while parked in front of a drug house, waiting on Letisha to score and come back out, I decided to get out and strike up a conversation with a couple of young black guys standing on the sidewalk. *What the Hell,* I thought, these guys have seen me around, they're probably cool. Maybe one of them can go inside and see what's holding my girl up, since she had warned me never to try and follow her inside this place. I figured they'd be friendly enough to talk to.

Not.

As I began approaching them, the taller of the young men gave a stern look and advised me, "You'd best get back in your car, sir." They both had their hands in their pockets; each wore the same red-colored sweat suits and matching doo-rags, and stood guard over the entry sidewalk to the drug house with wide stances, side by side.

I took another step, arms out and palms up, asking, "Hey, man, wassup, I was just won- …"

"I'm telling you, get back in your car, sir, and do *it now!*" the blank-faced tall man warned, this time with more volume and bite.

"Is there a problem?" I ventured, with another short step.

The shorter guy (who was still easily four inches taller and sixty pounds larger than me) started to lurch forward, but the voice halted him with one arm, and now he was pissed off, snapping at me, *"I'm only going to say this one more time: Get back in your car and stay there, man, or there's gonna to be trouble. You don' know where you are, and you don' wanna know. Get in you car.* ***NOW!"***

That was enough to elicit my fear and submission, but still I just shrugged nonchalantly, gave an insolent snort as I rolled my eyes with an arrogant turn of the head, and *strolled* (like I could care less and was completely unimpressed) back to the car, and sat inside, checking the rear view mirror, to see if the two of them were staying put. I *was* a bit scared but more disappointed; after all, I was just trying to be friendly. As I sat there fuming, Letisha suddenly reappeared, and as she bounced past my two "friends," she hollered, "Good lookin' out, dogs, thanks." She jumps in the car, instructing me, "Pull off, Marvin, quick." I hesitated, confused, started to ask what's the rush, but she practically shouts, *"Pull off, right now!"*

I did, and as we sped down the street, she explained that there was some trouble going on inside the house. An argument was becoming heated, a gunfight could break out and spread into the area any second now. When those places get that way, she said, anybody they don't know could be a suspect and a target for their hostility. I told her about the rude behavior of the "guard-dogs," and she just laughed and counseled me that here in the ghetto, that was their way of being nice to me. She had caught the tail end of my confrontation with them, knew right away what was happening, and that's why she had thanked them for the "good lookin' out," protecting me, really, from a situation that some green white guy from the suburbs could easily get hurt or killed in. The fact that they hadn't slapped me around, jacked me up for my money and *thrown* me back in the car was a testament to their good-natured and compassionate way of handling my naïve behavior.

I just shrugged and laughed it off outwardly, not wanting to appear uncool to Letisha, but inwardly I felt like an out-of-place fool who *should* have a lot more sensibility for a man of my age, especially since it wasn't like I had never hung out on the inner-city streets before, when I was younger. I knew it was the crack that was making me lose my senses, causing me to feel so invincible that I figured I could violate the unspoken laws of the underworld, desensitized to the harsh, vicious and unforgiving raw intensity of those who measure their manhood by the protection of their turf. I could never at the time admit it to myself, but I was turning into a stupid crackhead, and I *was* occasionally admonishing myself that I could very easily wind up as another dead statistic of street violence if I did not watch out.

I didn't pay any lengthy heed to my prudent pause, of course; the crack and the careless conduct kept coming, more and more, and more often than before, even after this warning episode. In-between highs, I was often terrified at what a precarious lifestyle I had fashioned for myself. I began having beastly dreams that would jolt me awake, sweating and shaking with fear, stark omens of doom in the night. I remember one such nightmare, in particular. I was in a familiar motel room with Letisha. She was sitting on the edge of the bed, with her back to me, undressing. Suddenly she turned toward me with a start, snarling, with dripping white fangs and the horned, fiery black diamond-eyed face of a crimson she-devil. I literally leaped out of bed, slapped myself in the face, and ran into the bathroom to splash cold water on my face. "I'm consorting with the devil!" I heard my own terrified voice.

Not that Letisha was really a devil, I knew; in fact, she

was just a poor hapless girl who had gotten caught up in the depraved world she lived in, succumbing to the enticing elixirs of pleasure that made life in the ghetto somewhat bearable, although profanely temporal and fatal. No, she was not a devil at heart, but evil *was* her course in life, and the realms of Satan were reaching me through my illicit relationship with her. As I stood naked in my washroom, thinking these things, I sobbed uncontrollably in grief, for her *and* me.

Whereas this whole affair had started out with me feeling like some kind of savior who could rescue this woman from a life of despair and hopelessness, now I had been drawn into the pitfalls of *her* world. There was nobody to blame but me; my predicament was no fault of Letisha's. I had made foolhardy decisions and choices, every step of the way, all on my own, with no gun held to my head. Worst of all, I was now starting to entertain the alarming *conscious* notion that I was indeed becoming a real drug addict. If that were true, I was powerless in any way to help even *myself*, let alone attempt to be some harbinger of the Promised Land for my destitute lady friend.

Over the course of about two or three months, the drug proved fatal to our ill-begotten love affair. Little by little, when I was not with Letisha, I started noticing that my desire for the crack was just as strong as, if not stronger than, my desire to be with her. I asked around and found a local dealer where I could score some stone for myself in-between dates with her. Within twelve weeks of my first hit, I was spending so much money on crack that I was rarely making the trip over to see and have a date with her anymore because I couldn't afford both.

My romance with the stone had developed into a stronger one than the romance with my girlfriend. Often she would call me and ask when I was coming over, wanting to see me again, missing me, wondering how I was doing. More often than not, I would make up some excuse as to why I couldn't come. I would hang up, feeling guilty about everything I could think of. "Well, isn't this just perfect," I lamented. "Now I'm even lying to *her* about where I am and what I'm doing!"

Worse still, I was now lying even to myself, *about* myself. I was in a desperate, conscious state of total denial. No way I could admit internally that I had become hopelessly addicted to crack. I could stop anytime I really wanted to, I told myself.

Eventually, the lies upon lies and my new "strange" behavior led to my exposure at home. I was in such a constant stupor that I couldn't keep my tracks covered accurately anymore. At one point during this period of time, and just before moving out, while driving together on the way home after a family picnic, my wife asked me if I had been seeing anyone else. Her tone of voice was a bit grave, and I knew that she knew.

During the picnic, I had snuck off several times to hit the pipe. I was still kind of high and just careless and reckless enough to admit that there *was* someone else. I mean, what was the point of keeping that secret anymore? When a woman's intuition strikes home, it is useless to continue to cover up, because you are doomed from the onset. I had learned that much in nearly 30 years of marriage.

She was crushed, hurt beyond belief, and my daughters were ready to castrate me. Until then, I had been putting up the front that I really wanted our relationship to work again and that the separation was a good idea to help "make our hearts grow fonder" of each other in the long run. All along I had held it in my mind that I could "have my cake and eat it, too," preserving the marriage for the sake of the family and keeping my mistress on the side. But now, she was insisting on a divorce, and I was beginning to panic. For a while, I nearly came to my senses. I realized I didn't *really* want to lose my wife forever over this recent selfish stupidity of mine, and I was not only in danger of losing her, but my entire family.

For a short time I even somehow managed to cut down on the dope a bit, enough to be able to carry on coherent discussions with my daughters and wife. We had all agreed to keep this from my son for the time being, because he is much bigger and stronger than me and has a rather volcanic temper. He had always been a "momma's boy," and even though he and I had always been close, we all feared he might attack me in his rage.

An agreement was struck. I was to give up the girlfriend and promise to never see her again. I deleted her number from my cell phone in front of my wife, and told her and both my daughters that I was ashamed and terribly sorry for having made this horrible and weak mistake. My wife was (incredibly) able to forgive me my transgressions and stated that *her* marriage vows were still intact and that if I would make good on my promise, there was still a chance for us to eventually get back together.

We agreed to see each other more often and go out on dates again, in an attempt to begin trying to rekindle the old flame. Both my daughters told her she was crazy for letting me off so easily, and they felt I should be made to suffer a long time before being forgiven. I had a long heart-to-heart talk with my son, gave him the whole story (about the affair, not the drug use). He took it rather well, and after the heavy part of the conversation was over, we wound up laughing and talking at length over a couple of beers.

As these talks continued, I was of course drilled with questions about my lover; how old she was, what she looked like, did she have any kids, what were her habits, her level of education, etc. During the inquisitions, I admitted to them that she was a crack user and that I had tried it "a couple of times" *(liar!)* but assured them I didn't really like the high and was not a user myself. That was a big mistake; neither my wife nor my daughters are stupid, and all three are endowed with SWI (Super Woman's Intuition). From that point on, my behavior was placed under microscopic scrutiny.

Of course my prudence was short-lived. I *was* a crackhead by this time, and the cravings kept on coming, and I kept on using. I had never completely stopped seeing Letisha, either, although as I said, it was much less frequently now. My habit had grown from a $20 rock two or three times weekly to $50 or $60 of dope per day by now. I was getting high every day and staying high, longer and longer, each day.

My family members started asking me if I was feeling all right, because I looked "different." They questioned me as to why I was losing so much weight, and I told them I was dieting. I was now living in a Hell of my own making. It cost me at least $50 a day in stone to just feel "straight." Without my daily fix, I couldn't concentrate enough to work and would get cold chill sweats and feel disoriented. Somehow, I was managing to get enough work done to get paid, and most of the money I earned was going into my ever-increasing addiction. Shortly after the third month anniversary of starting to use, the initial "harmless" flirtations with crack had grown into a full-blown $100-per-day habit. I got up every morning thinking about nothing except getting high; I spent the entire day trying to stay high, and I would sometimes go all night with no sleep, getting higher and higher.

You simply cannot hide this type of addiction from anyone who is close to you and loves you or even cares a little bit about you. Addicts can tell themselves that they are able to act straight and deceive others about their condition, but they really cannot. By this time my entire family knew I had a severe problem. Even worse, they knew that I was in denial about it and would probably be either dead or a broken-down homeless street person very shortly if nothing were done about it.

I remember one day, I had gotten the urge about mid-morning. I dropped my tools, leaving them in the front yard of the house where I was working as a carpenter, and (I found out later) leaving the front door to the clients' home wide open, with them having left for the day. I was driving to the neighboring city where my regular pickups were made, and it suddenly hit me. I heard a loud voice inside me, saying, ***"Marvin, admit it, you are a crackhead!"***

I trembled all over at the thought, the inner self-admission, but I continued on, driven by the craving for the dope. As I drove, I shed tears of shame over what I had become: a lying, cheating, hopeless drug addict who was not deserving of my loving, trusting, willing-to-forgive family. I didn't even deserve the affection of my illicit lover anymore; I was now betraying even the betrayal.

CHAPTER SEVEN

THE BETRAYAL OF GIBSON

I must digress for a moment and properly set the stage for this next dreadful telling. You see, before I became lost to myself, before the alien had cocooned in my guts, fed on my heart, and ripped its way to life through my chest cavity, killing its host in the process, I had precious people and things in my life, that I loved dearly. One of those loves was music.

I was *born* with the gift of music. At the age of two, I gave my first public performance, standing on the piano bench in church, next to my mother, who accompanied me as I sang, "Give Me that Old Time Religion." By the time I was in high school, I could play the bass fiddle, guitar and some piano. I was voted student president of the choir, and was writing and arranging musical scores, and landing lead roles in the annual musical theater productions. I was able to go to college on a music scholarship and was beginning to flex my musical muscles in the classical genre, composing some pieces which were regarded highly enough by my professors to get included on the programs of public recitals. This was all before I got "tuned in, turned on, and dropped out" with the whole hippie thing.

As a hippie, I was immediately drawn to the musical side of the movement, no surprise, and soon found myself in the market for an electric guitar. I wanted to be a lead guitar rock and roll player, like Jimmy Hendrix, Eric Clapton or Carlos Santana. I didn't have much money, but by good fortune, I ran into a local high school kid who had an old 1952 Gibson Les Paul, vintage, mind you, mint condition, and he was willing to let it go for a pound of weed. I was not a dealer, but I had buddies who could get that kind of weight, so I was able to set up the deal. I purchased a pound of Columbia's finest. Back then the price was $75. I took the package over to the kid's house at an agreed-upon time when his parents would not be there and bartered the reefer for the guitar.

Everyone who knew anything about guitars told me what a steal I had gotten in this deal. This was a collector's item, something to be respectful of, should only be played by someone who appreciates quality craftsmanship, and definitely held onto forever. Taking the advice of a friend who was an accomplished player and knew a lot about how to produce the "now" sounds of popular rock and roll, I had it modified with stronger "hum-bucker" pickups, rewired for in- and out-of-phase sounds, and fitted with state-of-the-art tuning pegs and a tune-a-matic bridge. Even on my low-budget beginner's amplifier, it had a sound that was magnificent, powerful and full. I played it from early morning until late in the evening nearly every day for six months, as I taught myself how to play the popular "licks" of the big-name recording artists. Seven months after acquiring this treasure, I landed my first gig as a lead guitarist in a band that was rehearsing its show, getting ready to hit the road with several months of bookings all set up. It was the summer of 1970, and I was in love with my Les Paul, and he loved me back.

Together, we set out to change the world with original music, written by me, played upon Les. I would occasionally buy and try out other guitars just for variety of sound in performances, but none of them ever stuck with me for very long. No, it was Les and I, going all the way. When a song needed true passion and the screaming voice of my generation, I always turned to old faithful, my first love, my one and only Gibson Les Paul. Les was the guitar I was playing when I first met my wife-to-be in a nightclub. The date had been pre-arranged by my drummer, who knew my taste in women and had told a cousin of his to come out and catch the show, telling her she should get a load of the hot guitar player in his band.

When first he pointed her out to me, I was awestruck. She was *stunningly* beautiful and exuded enough sexuality to make a man's knees buckle … the kind of drop-dead gorgeous that reaches the point of intimidating. Really … I mean, looks that good should be illegal. You should have to carry a license or something. Any average Joe checking out a babe like that would've been daunted to the point of needing to get drunk before mustering up enough temerity to dare approach her, but I had a secret weapon. I had my good buddy Les. Les and I knew what we had to do, and we did it in bold and grand fashion. We lit the house up that night, and by midway through the evening she was giving me that look. You know, that look a woman gives a man when she's letting him know that she thinks he *really is* all that. I was feeling rather proud and lucky, to say the least, but I've got to give up the props to Les. To this day, I'm quite sure if I hadn't had him enhancing my game, I'd have never been able to leave the club that night with her phone number in my pocket and an invitation to dinner at her place the next day.

Les and I traveled everywhere together; he slept next to my bed at night, was always in the seat next to mine on the bus, and even after I got married, had one kid and another on the way, and had to leave the rock and roll nightlife to get a "real job" to better support my young family, he was always there in my life. When I was frustrated or down, I could always pull old Les out of the closet, play a few tunes, and feel comforted and better. Sometimes I would just *look* at the guitar and get this warm feeling, a reunion with happy memories. For more than 30 years this love affair flourished, and I never once failed to appreciate my friend Les, who had been through so much with me and had always been there for me.

That was then. That's all over now, because I sold the useless piece of crap.

Let me tell you something about crackheads. We don't think straight. We are not loyal, not to anyone, not to anything. We do not *care* about anything, except getting high. We use crack logic when we make our decisions. *Crack logic*, do you understand? It's an oxymoron, with the emphasis on moron. You want more on this? Here ya go.

One day I wake up. I'm in the basement. My wife has just moved out … I'm all alone. I need to smoke some stone. I don't have any. I need some money to get some stone. I don't have any.

I start thinking about what I can do to get some money. I'm in-between jobs, haven't had a paycheck in over two weeks, and won't get another check until I can start the next job. That's more than a week away. I'm already overextended on my credit line with my dealer. I've been selling stuff to get by. I've already sold the guitar my wife bought me for Christmas a few years before, even though it was a fine, expensive, professional quality, hollow-body Yamaha with built-in electric pickup and equalizer, well worth keeping. My crack logic told me that since she was gone now, and my hands had so much arthritis in them I rarely even picked up and played a guitar any more anyway, it would be better to sell it and get some money, so I could ease the physical and emotional pain I was in by smoking some crack.

I received $150, selling the guitar my wife had paid $1,000 for, and it was still in perfect condition. By the end of that same day, the $150 had been smoked up, and gone forever was the gift from my once-beloved life partner.

The house was nearly barren by now. I had sold the stove, refrigerator and dishwasher, pawned a few sporting goods I had, my guitar amplifier, speaker cabinet, microphone, mike stand, effects pedal, and any carpentry tools I did not absolutely have to have in order to perform my job, as well as any jewelry of value I had left. When my wife moved out, she had taken nearly all the furniture, leaving me a futon couch to sleep on and a recliner, along with a small eating table, a couple of chairs and a TV. I didn't care about the emptiness of the house, except for the fact that I was now getting desperate for saleable items. Keeping up with a $100-a-day habit, with no money and no income, poses a bit of a challenge for someone like me.

So this day when I wake up, I happen to remember old Les, who so far, had managed somehow, to escape from my ravenous selling spree. He was in hiding in the guest bedroom closet. My crack logic helps me once again to make the right decision. It was going to be tough, but it was time to sell Les. Yep, my mind was made up, as hard as it would be to part company with such a good old friend, it was definitely better for the both of us. After all, I wasn't playing guitar anymore; my hands ached too much. I wasn't doing Les any favors by keeping him in a dark closet. He deserved to be played! It would be better to set him free; allow some young player to be able to make him sing again. Better for old Les, and better for me. I need the money. I take the tattered, road-worn case out of the closet, open it up, and close it back again, quickly. I don't want to pick him up or try to finger the frets one last time. This is no time for sentiment. I have to be firm, because this is going to be hard enough as it is. And better. It will be better this way. That's what my crack logic tells me. I carry the guitar out to my car and drive off to a store that pays cash for saleable used instruments.

As I think back on it, this was how I was losing my family and everyone in my life who loved and cared about me. None of them had stopped loving me, but I had driven them away. This was the same old Les that I had loved for so long, and had felt loved back by him for just as long, that like them, now had to go.

I hadn't stopped loving Les, or any of them, either, but my love and need for crack was the strongest thing in my life now, and crack is a jealous lover. She doesn't want any competition. She wants you all to herself, and if anyone comes between you and her, she will make sure you sell them out, betray them, double-cross them, cheat and lie to them, ignore them, do anything you need to do, to get them out of your life, because there's no time, and no room, for anything, or anyone else, when crack is your mistress and master.

One memory that will always haunt me as a hallmark of those heinous days is of parting company with my son, one summer day, after work. He didn't have a car at the time, so I was in the habit of picking him up in the morning and dropping him off at his job. He was working as a carpenter. Like me, he is gifted with an aptitude for making and crafting things. Whenever he couldn't get a ride home after work from someone he was working with, he would call me, and I would pick him up and take him home. This day, I had gotten the call, and when I arrived at his job, he was standing in front of the house being remodeled, with his tool belt strung over his shoulder.

As soon as he spotted me, his face lit up with that huge, genuine, infectious smile of his. I had seen that smile thousands of times during his 21 years of life. It was the smile he got whenever he saw his dad and knew that dad was going to spend some time with him. We always did things together as he was growing up. Cub scouts, basketball practice, Aikido lessons, making things in my woodworking shop, building forts in the snow, having snowball fights, arm wrestling, teaching him how to drive a stick shift, building perfect campfires, all the great guy things a son and father can and love to do. He was the only other male in the house, and I've had a special bond with him ever since his birth. My wife has always reminded me of the unforgettable look of joy I had on my face when he was born, and I saw it was a boy; my son had finally been given to me.

We talked and laughed on the way over to his apartment, discussing the day's work and just little things, nothing heavy. As we approach his place, however, I notice a change in his attitude. I could sense he didn't want to get out of the car and go inside his empty apartment. His roommates had gone out, there was nothing to do in there but watch some boring TV, and he had no vehicle with which to go visit a friend. My first thought told me, *now* would be the perfect time to ask him if he would like to hang out with me for the evening. It had been a long time since we had spent any length of quality time together, and I knew he would be delighted at the thought of Dad taking some time out with him, chumming like we used to do so often. I almost start to get the words out, but then I realized …

I couldn't do it.

I knew I wouldn't be able to be with him for long, before my addiction kicked back in and I'd have to get high, and I can't do that when I'm around him. I had half an eight ball in my pocket, and the crack logic was scolding me for even *entertaining* the notion of spending time with my son, rather than occupying the rest of the evening with getting stoned.

As I watched him meandering up the walk to his apartment, sloped shouldered, looking to me depressed and lonely, I could only imagine that what he really wanted was to turn around and ask me if I would like to come in for a while, hang out for a bit with him. But he didn't; he knew by then that he couldn't ask that. He's no fool, and he, like all the rest of the family, knew that his once-attentive, loving and doting father and friend now had a life that did not include very much time with him any more. Bitter with myself, grief-stricken and ashamed, I pulled away, leaving him alone, heading off by myself to smoke my crack.

With that vivid memory chastising what's left of my conscience, I now pull into the parking lot of the secondhand music store. Time to betray, and part company, with Les, just like all the rest.

I know that this act is just another nail in the coffin, another stamp of the death sentence I am delivering to everyone and everything I had once held dear. Whereas I used to enjoy listening to, reading, writing and playing music, I no longer care for any of those things. I used to be an insatiable reader, devouring book after book, deriving endless pleasure from the stretches of imagination and information they gave me. Books are useless to me now; I can't sit still, or focus long enough, to enjoy them. All my other hobbies and interests, sports, camping, playing cards, woodworking, writing poems and stories, are all gone to me; just like all my family and friends. They would still be with me if I could let them, but I don't have the time, interest, or ability to include them in my daily regimen, which consists entirely now, of doing *only* that which makes it possible to stay high. Everything else has to go.

It is a spiritually dried-up, companionless loner who is getting out of the car, obeying his unquenchable thirst for estrangement.

I walk into the store, case in hand. I feel like a pet parent who is having his faithful, tired old dog put to sleep; like a homeless single parent who is putting his child up for adoption because he is an incapable and unfit father. Nevertheless, I force myself up to the counter and start talking turkey with the salesman.

He tells me that this particular guitar has very little resale value. Because of the modifications I had made to it, even though it was over 50 years old and in excellent condition, it does not qualify as a classic collector's item. He suggests that this instrument, obviously customized for a working musician, would be better sold through ads in the paper or on eBay, somewhere where a real player could recognize its value and pay me the tall dollar. He apologizes that he cannot offer me very much for it because, he explains, his store caters to beginner musicians and collectors, neither of whom would pay much for this particular kind of "off-beat" guitar.

Now I am in a dilemma. What he is saying makes sense; it is sound thinking, complete with a logical solution to my problem. A little patience, and with proper marketing, this fine old pal could find a proper new home, and I would get far more money for it than I can get here and now. That is completely un-crack-like-logic, however, and does me no good because I need whatever I can get, *right now.*

I mutter some lying cockamamie story about needing to leave town, trying to lighten up the traveling gear, blah-blah-blah stuff, that is of no concern to him, and tell him that regardless of what price the guitar might fetch on the open market, I am ready to deal with him, here and now. "Give me your best shot," I say.

In the end, I wind up selling my 1952 Gibson Les Paul, my close friend for my entire adult life, for a mere $75, the same price I had paid for it 35 years before. Back then, I had traded weed to a pothead for it, $75 worth. I had thought the young kid was a fool for letting it go so cheap. Now, I was the *old* fool, letting go of it for just as cheap, having vastly degraded it in value by my crack addiction's voracious and niggardly impatient appetite. The pothead had had a father who apparently didn't know his son well enough to be aware of what he was doing with his money and time. The crackhead selling the guitar now, had a son who knew very little of what his father was doing anymore, either. Such irony. Seventy-five dollars. From a pothead to a crackhead, with three and a half decades in between, and right back to the same seventy-five dollars we come.

It was as though nothing of importance or value had ever happened, during all that time.

I take the check from the unconcerned man, feeling like Judas after accepting the 30 pieces of silver, in return for betraying his best friend and Master. I get out of there quickly and slump into my car. Like Judas, I was only fit to be stoned and ready to get on with hanging myself. I pull out my pipe and stare at it. The grim thought rumbles and thunders through my skull,

"Behold, the noose of Judas!"

CHAPTER EIGHT

"PICKING UP" ON THE ROMANCE (A DAY IN THE LIFE OF A CRACKHEAD)

So now I'm on my way to work, late as usual, and ripped out of my gourd. I haven't driven more than five minutes when the urge to fire up hits me again, so I pull over into another parking lot, light up, and feel the euphoric relief enveloping my body and mind. Looking at my heater, I see that there are lots of residual narcotics built up on the inside of the stem, so I push the char back and forth several times, allowing the copper mesh to gather the dope into another pretty good bonus load, and fire up again. Through the mystical blue-gray haze of hell's paradise fogging the windshield, my eyesight cracks an opening out into the real world, gazing wistfully at normal people. They're shopping, walking their dogs, scolding their kids, chatting, laughing, seemingly happy. Not like me. Without motivation or reason, I decide to drive some more.

The drive to work should only take about fifteen minutes from where I'm staying, but it takes me 45 minutes to get there because I keep stopping every few minutes to reload and keep the high going. Finally, around 11:30 a.m., I get to the job, take another hit, and get out of the car, struggling to look and walk straight, hoping the clients are not home. I hack away for a couple of hours, trying to ignore the urge to take a break and resume smoking, fighting with all my might to concentrate enough to do reasonably good work.

By early afternoon I start feeling disoriented again and head back to my vehicle to take a break and get my high going. I pull out the tiny tinfoil package and unfold it, and groan to myself when I see that my big rock is now just a little pebble, maybe enough for one or two good hits, that's all. I quickly smoke that and decide it would be best to drive back over and hook up with my dealer right now, so I can get back and get some more work done before the end of the day. So back I go to the 'hood, wasting gas, wasting time, and wasting my already wasted mind.

I try calling my dealer but start panicking when I keep getting his answering service. What if he isn't around? What do I do then? I know of several other dealers, but I don't know if I can trust them. I have been ripped off before, and I had struck an exclusive deal with my main man; me promising to only pick up with him, he promising to always "be there" for me and even drop me some rock on credit, sometimes even for free, if I needed it. Yes, crack can be had with credit, if your payment history is good enough. It's just like the old credit card game: Pay your bills on time, borrow more each time, and the credit limits will keep going up. The higher the limit, the more you spend. The more you spend, the higher the limit, and so on.

Smart dealers understand the marketing magic of the "loss-leader" principle, also. If a customer has a $20 daily habit, give him or her an extra free 20 once or twice, pretty soon you've got a $40-a-day client. Repeat this process over and over, and although you give up some product along the way, you've got a big-spending customer forever, or at least until the imbecile goes broke, crashes and burns. This sound business practice works remarkably well, especially when your merchandise is a powerfully addictive narcotic.

So anyway, I'm back at it again; the credit game, but instead of spending more money than I've earned, now I'm smoking dope before I've paid for it. With each week, as my habit grows, when payday comes on Friday, more and more of my check is already tagged for payment of my drug debt. By now, the majority of my weekly earnings are gone the day I get my paycheck, and within a day or two, I am back to buying dope on credit for the rest of the week. My dealer takes his money very seriously, and I have heard all the horror stories of what can happen to druggies who don't pay on time and/or who double-cross their dealers.

I usually manage to keep *some* cash on me, however, and I am seriously willing to take any risk necessary to score if I can't get with my man. Scoring from someone else isn't exactly a double-cross, it's more of an undercut, and I've done some favors for him before, so I'm not worried too much about giving someone else a little business if he isn't available at the time. Still, I'm feeling a bit nervous about the whole situation.

Fortunately, my phone rings and it's him, relieving my angst. "Watcha need, my brotha?" comes the silky deep voice that already knows the answer. I come back with, "Hey, dog, need some more work; hook me up with a bill; I'll be straight for the day." "Where you at?" he wants to know, and I shoot back, "five minutes out, holla atcha when I'm gettin' short." His "Fo' sho" gets clipped off by the snap of the cell phone.

I make the pickup with no problems, and my dealer does me a big favor, selling me a whole "eight ball" for my $100. An eight ball is a crackhead's dream-stone, about the size of a grape tomato. It's enough dope to get two or three people high for a whole day and usually sells on the street for around $200. I do the usual stop; get-high-and-go, stutter-drive back to work. I make a feeble attempt at finishing the day's project, but by 4:00 in the afternoon, I'm ready to pack it in for the day and get on with some serious smoking. I tidy up the worksite in a hurry, hop in my car, have another hit for the road, and head toward my house.

Maybe I should get something to eat, I think to myself. As I drive along, looking at the fast food restaurants, though, the thought of eating has no appeal. The rock in my pants pocket is calling me, so I head straight for my house. I don't like driving high on crack. It's not fun or comfortable, because I am continuously paranoid. I always think cops are looking at me, that they are sizing me up, about to pull me over. I feel like people are staring at me strangely. Sudden noises, noises that are actually normal on the streets, make me jump in my seat. Besides going to work and making the drive to score another pickup, I like to stay primarily at home, a lonesome loner.

That's what happens to drug addicts. They pull back from contact with other people. Preferring to be alone, not having to lie to anyone, or put on a straight act, and needing the solitude in order to pursue my new-found love, I now spend most of my time by myself. No family, no friends, I don't want them around. Not because I don't love my family, but because I am so ashamed of what I have become and at the same time so hooked on the dope I can't be around them for any length of time without needing to sneak off somewhere and get a quick fix. And then, I have to go back around them and try and act straight, knowing that they probably know I am high again, creating that awkward feeling between everyone. My TV is broke, and I don't even miss it enough to spend the money to have it fixed or replaced. Gone are the days when I can entertain myself with a good book. All I want to do with my time is get high.

I pull into my driveway, smiling. Safe at home, nobody to bother me, and a whole eight ball to smoke. It is going to be a great night! I go in, lock the door behind me, and begin immediately prepping my heater, cutting the treasured stone into rations that should last me well into tomorrow, with no need to go anywhere or do anything but smoke crack. I prep some fresh char and bite off the damaged end of the heater with my teeth. The intense fire cracks the end of the glass tube over time, and you have to keep removing the broken portion of the stem as necessary. This stem has plenty of length left for the evening, so

I tamp the new char into it, load up a good portion of stone, pour myself a tall vodka on the rocks, and sit back in my easy chair, ready to begin a long evening of nothing but smoking and letting my imagination run wild.

I smoke and smoke and smoke. I get so high, I'm in a faraway, different world. It's a better world. A heavenly domain, in which I can do anything, be anybody I want to. I am charming, handsome, youthful, strong, wealthy and powerful. So strange is this high that these feelings can overcome and bolster me, even while simultaneously realizing that I'm an idiotic fool, tied to a crack pipe. Somehow, it doesn't matter. As long as I can stay in my fantasy world and feel this good, I am OK, and everything is wonderful. Only when the stone runs out am I miserable, and when that happens, I am *very* miserable.

Night falls. Time and care have long since evaporated, so much so that I am nearing the end of my eight ball and don't even know it. I walk back into the kitchen where I keep my stash, pull out the bag, and I can't believe my eyes … I'm almost out of stone! One little load left. Damn! I look at my watch; midnight … not too late to drive back over and score a nightcap, I think. I call my dealer. No answer. I'm getting desperate; I need more stone to keep this high going and avoid a crash. Too high to go to sleep, and unwilling to face coming down just yet, I rush out to my car and head back over to the 'hood, ready to take my chances and get some rock any way that I can. I am insanely high, looking for some wild adventure.

Repeatedly on the way over, I keep calling my dealer, but no answer. *That's all right,* I think, I know where I can go to cop this time of night. I turn onto the strip, where I know a couple of hookers who can score for me if I give them a tip. By now, I know all the hot spots, so I pull behind a certain gas station and wait, checking out the sidewalks and streets. Hip-hop, thunder-decibel, hydraulic-rap cars cruise by, with thug-looking drivers and wannabe passengers, tossing beer cans out the window, sporting attitudes and joints. It's a hot midnight hour, so I roll down the window, smelling the pungent asphalt atmosphere; tonight it's laced with electricity and the macabre, intoxicating, excitement of jeopardy.

I see a familiar girl who's done several pickups for me before. She's swaying along the street-side, swishing her derriere, calling out and waving "come-on" signs to men driving by. She must be barely 20 years old, but I know this chick to be wilder than an atomic bomb in the wrong hands and typically higher than Jupiter. Tonight, she's red-dressed for undressing, dripping with salaciousness, and in *rare* form, even for her. As I observe her, all mouthy and trash-talking, working the street, I feel a bizarre combination of melancholy and desire. She spots me, gets a grin on, waves and jogs over, entering my car with, "Yo, whassup, baby?"

A memory of the first time I saw her zips through my brain. It was breakfast-time at a Coney Island, and she was slumped over her eggs, alone, with a black hoodie on, covering most of her sobbing face, in a booth at the back. I recalled how I had felt sad for her and had asked her what was wrong, on my way to the men's room. She had looked up defiantly at me and rasped out, "What the fuck does it matter to you?" I had said nothing, attempted a perfunctory smile and posture of sympathy, but left her alone, feeling even more sorry for her, yet helpless in the face of a stranger's despair.

The next time we had met, it was weeks later, on a night when I had been drinking heavily, needing to get out of the house, away from my nagging wife and an escalating argument. I had driven by this very corner and spotted her doing her thing as a whore. I had slowed down to get a better look. She had the liar's false grin and street-swagger bravado thing going on then, strengthened in attitude by intoxicants, raising hell and doing it well. She suddenly recognized me, approached my car, and knocked on my window, anticipating a date. Just then a cop car had turned the corner. I got scared, shook my head "no" and drove off.

Since then, however, we had several encounters, although never sexual. In my inverted, and perverted, moral code at the time, I was still being faithful to my girlfriend. Letisha had taught me that hookers could score dope for you. In fact, that had been her favorite way of getting money out of guys without having to "put out." You ask the John if he'd like to get high first, he'd usually agree, you'd cop some stone for him (at his expense, of course), encourage him to get blasted, and before he knew it, he was not so much interested in sex, as he was in getting some more rock. Smoke too much crack, and a man's sex drive goes limp; that was a trade technique that "smart" whores used, her sister had mentored her. This took more *time* than turning a quick sex trick, of course, but usually with all the scoring tips and "money-meter" charges ("my time is money, honey"), you could make out fine without having to screw the idiot.

So after developing my own crack habit, in between dates with Letisha, I had begun looking this local girl up occasionally for that reason. I could tell she liked me, probably because I talked to her as a person, not as a piece of meat. She had told me her name was Brandy.

Now here Brandy is in my car again, and "Cop me a fifty, doll; you know I'll take care 'ya," comes out of my mouth. She asks to use my phone, makes a call, and then says, "OK, sweetie, we gotsta go over to the Highway House; you know where that's at?" "Fo' sho," I say and pull out into traffic.

The Highway House is hotter than Hell, a drug *and* whorehouse where crack is cooked *and* sold, and you can also get any other illegal drug you want there: meth, ecstasy, heroin, weed, uppers, downers, you name it. You can get your "freak" on and get your high on at the same place. Even prescription drugs, like Vicadin, Viagra and Levitra, can be gotten there. Yes, the young bucks in the 'hood like to enhance their bedroom performances with drugs these days. I can only imagine how sexually flaccid these guys will be as middle-aged men, after several decades of dependence on artificial stimulation. Then again, old age is not something you think or care about in this world. It's all about *now* and what can you get or do to make you feel happy and powerful *right now*.

As we approach the Highway House, Brandy tells me to park inconspicuously a block or so down from the front, which I already knew well enough to do from previous escapades with Letisha. By now, I'm well aware that unknown middle-aged white guys are not the most welcomed guests in places like these. In fact, they are marks, often mugged and robbed, especially this time of night. You can get inside if you want to buy a girl and are accompanied by a pimp they know and trust; but only the hookers, pimps and dealers can come and go as they please, dropping off money, and taking drugs out of the house. Brandy takes my money, including her $10 tip, gets out, and walks up to the two story dilapidated house that looks like it *might* have been painted white back when it still had paint on it. She says something to a mammoth black dude sitting on the front porch (who is obviously a lookout for heat); he casts a somber glance my way, turns back, and nods his huge goateed head at her. She disappears inside.

Good lookin' out, girl, I think to myself, remembering the teachings of Letisha. I knew she had just made sure the house guard would be watching over me, ensuring I would still be here, in one piece, when she comes back out. I stay in my car, like a good little white boy. I wait, 10, maybe 15, minutes, and I'm starting to get impatient. It shouldn't take this long for a pre-scheduled pickup, and I'm worried about cops circling the area, distant, but still too close for comfort. Finally, I see her coming out the front door; she skips over to my car and pops in. She's all gushy and happy, and handing me my dope, says, "Just made me some *fast* money, dog. Had this trick inside waitin' on me; he pumps me 'bout three times, gets off like this (pops her fingers), gives me fitty dollas. Woo-hoo! Take me up to the store, OK, honey?" "Fershizzle," I say, and off we go.

We get to the convenience store, and I ask her what she wants, my treat. She asks for a Pepsi and a bottle of water. I get the stuff, also picking up a new rose stem for myself, come back to the car and give her the drinks. She asks, "All right if I shoot up here before I get out?" "No problem, babe," I say. She takes out her works (paraphernalia) and proceeds to heat some heroin in a spoon of water, load the mix in a syringe, band off her forearm, locate a blood vein, and shoot up. She falls back in the seat, moaning in ecstasy. I keep my eye out for cops.

After several minutes of gazing off into space, she comes back to reality, puts her hand on the door handle, then hesitates, turns to me with a devilish smile, and asks, "Sure you don't wanna getcher freak on with me this time, baby? Give you some free pussy if you share some stone with me." For a moment *I am tempted*. But I like this girl. In a strange and ironic way, I even *care* about her, and I wish that somehow I were a better man who could help her and not contribute any more (than I already have) to her lost life and self-demeaning ways. Somewhere, from deep inside me, there comes a little (but firm) voice of goodness that tells me to say, "No, babe, ain'bout that wichyou & me, know'm sayin'?" She leans over, kisses me on the cheek, opens the door, gives me a wink, and slow-drawls, "Aau-right, stay cool, baby … you *know* you *my* nigger." "Word," I say, and as she heads back onto the street, I head for the expressway, driving back home alone, with a fresh stone to smoke.

When I get back, it's around 2:00 a.m. *It's a Thursday*

night, gotta work tomorrow, and I should be trying to get some sleep, I think to myself. But instead, I pull out my new stem, prep the char, load up my new heater, and fire it up. After a few more pulls, I'm starting to hallucinate. The ceiling turns into a clear blue sky, with birds flying by and clouds forming images of miraculous Gods and friendly angels. I look out the patio door and see the moon in the sky; it's dancing and changing colors, appearing ominously close and then so far away it's like a pencil dot being consumed by emptiness. Suddenly I hear a "*RAP!*" on the window. I'm sure I see my wife, standing outside looking in, trying to locate me. *"Oh, God, no!"* I panic, bolt out of my chair, and head for the kitchen to try and hide my works before she knocks on the door. Then I realize I was just getting paranoid again, chuckle to myself, load another hit up since I'm in there anyway, pour another drink, and head back to my easy chair.

Outside I hear a siren. I panic again, thinking for sure it's the cops. They must have tailed me from the Highway House and are about to break in and bust me! But the sound goes on by, fades away, and I sigh in relief and reload for another hit.

By 5:00 a.m. I'm out of stone again. Too late for another run, and out of money and credit anyway, I decide to try and get a little sleep before having to go to work. I've spent $200 in the past 18 hours, consumed more than $300 worth of crack, while throwing back a fifth and a half of vodka, and I'm blitzed beyond sanity.

I take off my clothes, lie in the bed, try closing my eyes, but I'm starting to sweat and I'm twitching all over. I feel cold, and my head is spinning. No use trying to sleep, I think, after 20 minutes or so of futile effort, so I get up. There's nothing to do, I'm not hungry, my high is coming down, and I'm feeling restless. I decide to look for some stone fragments. Maybe I can scrape up enough specks to have another hit.

I go into the kitchen, naked, and start crawling around on the floor, looking for bits and pieces that may have fallen off the counter. Sure enough, I find plenty of stone to make up a couple loads. I fire up, feeling the ecstasy one more time. After another last search on the floor for one more possible load, and finding nothing worth smoking, I give up, moan to myself, and stumble back to the bed with my head spinning. After glancing at the clock and reading 6:15 a.m., I lie down and pass out immediately.

The next thing I know my alarm is sounding. Time to get up. It's 7:30 a.m. My first thought is, *Fuck! Oh, God, no, not another day already!* Desperately I search all my stash spots and look everywhere in the house for some stone I may have left over from last night. Nothing. I search all my clothes pockets from yesterday and the day before. Nothing again. I go outside and search the car. Nada. "Damn," I say out loud, "Why the Hell can't I ever leave any rock for in the morning?" It's Friday, I'm out of cash, I don't get my check until around noon, and it's way too early to score any dope, anyway.

Somehow, someway, I'm going to have to try and gut it out for five or six hours before I can get straight. The high is gone, and I'm feeling sweaty, shaky and disoriented. I take a cold shower, fix a quick egg sandwich for breakfast, and force it down with a cup of coffee. I jump in my car and start driving to the job.

I'm feeling lonely, depressed, full of anxiety, and scared. I begin to cry as I drive along, slowly and surely having to admit to myself that I am now a slave to this stuff and that my Master will be calling on me and demanding my submissive service all the live-long day. My life has become nothing more than a useless waste of time, and I know it's going to be just --

another Goddamn day in the life of a crackhead.

CHAPTER NINE

THIS IS ALL JUST A BAD DREAM, RIGHT?

Part One: The Internal Dialogue (three months in)

Q: Have you lost your mind? Are you crazy?
A: No, this can't be me. I'm not this kind of person. All I have to do is get off the dope.

Q: You *can't* get off the dope, you idiot; you're hooked!
A: No, I am *NOT* hooked. I'm going to quit … I'll cop today, and that will be it. I'm getting off this shit for good tomorrow.

Q: You're a damn fool and a liar, too. You've made that promise to yourself many times, and you *KNOW* you can't keep it. ***FACE IT, MARVIN: YOU ARE A DEAD MAN WALKING!***
A: Shut up … *shut up…* ***SHUT THE FUCK UP!!***

Q: So just what are you really going to do about it? How long do you think you can go on like this? Another month? A year? Two?
A: I don't know. This doesn't seem real. It has to be a nightmare. I must be dreaming. Dear God, please let this be a dream; it's just a horrible nightmare, right?

Q: Wrong, fool, you made every choice and every decision that got you here, you wretched waste of human flesh. You really thought you could dance all night and not have to pay the fiddler? Hey, Mr. Believes in and has always taught the Universal Law of

Karma, did you think the rules didn't apply to you?

A: Stop tormenting me, please; just let me have some peace. I'm already miserable enough. Oh, God, I just want to kill myself and end it all right now.

Q: Go ahead, *do it!* You think that will end it all? You know better than that, chump. *Pull the trigger, motherfucker!* You got Hell to pay, so why not get started? You're in Hell right now anyway, aren't you? Nobody gives a shit about you, including yourself, right?

A: No, that's not right. I mean yes, I *am* in Hell, and I *don't* care about myself anymore, but I've got a wife and a family that needs me.

Q: *Needs* you? Needs ***You?***

A: No, not this me, the other guy; the man I used to be, before this thing I'm looking at started calling itself me.

Q: You are a hopeless lost soul. You are beyond any hope of salvation, and your family will *never* treat you the same even if you *were* able to quit, which you *are not able to do* anyway. They will *never* be able to trust you or respect you in any way, *ever again*. Don't you realize that by now?

A: But they're telling me they do love me, and they want me to quit so they can have me back again, be whole again, be the husband, father and grandfather again.

Q: You stupid dumbshit, you buying that? YOU?

A: I want to, yes. I so desperately want to believe it.

Q: Enough to go cold turkey and turn yourself in for treatment?

A: Yes, pretty soon. I know I have to go through the fire sooner or later.

Q: When are you going to do it?

A: It won't be long, it can't be. I know that. I'll die and be lost in satanic realms of the underworld with not enough self-will to make it back to life if I don't overcome this bad karma before my physical death.

Q: Nice thoughts, great intentions … *WHEN?*
A: Soon. It's going to be soon. It has to be.

On and on this tormenting internal dialogue would replay itself in my mind, over and over, in looped repeat mode. I was powerless to stop it. Once a Zen student with the ability to focus my mind and reach states and levels of higher consciousness by stilling the inner dialogue and tapping into universal consciousness, I now had the attention span of a mosquito, and a brain that ruled me and tortured me.

The *only* way out of the nightmare of my consciousness was to go back into the main character of the dream and get lost in the horrible "now" of my life again. That is, get high. Get high enough that the drug can transform the nightmare into a party that's so much fun, you can't imagine what you had ever been worried about. It was a drug-induced schizophrenia, I suppose. I'm no psychologist, but I definitely seemed to have two distinctly different personalities that were trying to kill each other.

One day, my wife called me on my cell phone. I was high but not so out of it that I couldn't carry on a reasonably coherent conversation, so when I saw her number on the ID panel, I answered. She wanted to talk. She said it was important and couldn't wait. She was coming right over to pick me up, and she wanted me to come with her, to her place, so we could sit together and talk about it right now.

Something inside told me that this was the moment of reckoning, and for some strange reason, a part of me was ready for it. Even though I thought I heard someone else say it, and

I didn't know if I agreed with that person, I distinctly heard someone who sounded just like me say, "OK, sure; come on over. I'm at home."

Part Two: Trying to Wake Up

I didn't know it yet, but my wife was about to save my life. She pulled up in the drive, I smiled and got in her car, and we headed off for her condo. I asked what was so important that we needed to talk about, but she said she would prefer to wait until we could sit down face to face and discuss the matter. So we spent the 15-minute drive in idle chitchat; you know, "so how you doing?" "Oh, not too bad, how have you been?" and so forth.

I knew what the real conversation was going to be about, of course. A month prior, she had popped in on me on a whim one evening, just to say "hi" and see how I was doing. She had caught me red-handed, sitting in my living room in my easy chair, naked, right in the act of taking a long pull on my pipe. By then, I had gotten so sloppy with my cover-up act that I had left the patio door wide open, and she had walked straight in, unannounced, before I knew what was happening. She had blown up in rage, shouting at me that I was an idiot, a fool, and screamed at me that I was going to go down and lose everything. She had stormed out of the house, taking my pipe with her, pausing to throw it on the brick pavers and smash it with her foot. She had jumped in her car, slammed the door, and squealed out of the parking lot. Within minutes, she called me on my cell phone and told me, with a hysterical high-pitched voice, that she wanted a divorce and that I would never see my kids or grandchildren again; they would no longer have anything to do with me.

The next morning, however, she had called me again. She had calmed down by then and confessed to me that she hadn't slept all night, thinking and worrying about me, and she told me she wanted to help me. "No way in Hell" was she going to allow some filthy drug to take her husband's life, she said. That's just the kind of woman my wife is. She reacts spontaneously, honestly and openly when she's disgusted with someone or something, blurts out her emotions, even to the point of violent behavior and raging dialogue, then contemplates and meditates over the matter, calms down, and comes back with a strength and resolve to rectify and/or heal the person or situation in any way she can.

She had gone through this same cycle when I confessed to her that I had been seeing another woman. For several days, whenever we would see each other, she did nothing but scream at me, slap me in the face, and even broke into my bedroom one night, woke me up, shaking me and slapping me around so tough, I had bruises all over my body for several days after. But within a week, she had found it in herself to forgive me and had committed to trying to work out our differences and saving our marriage if at all possible. The woman has strength, compassion, integrity, honesty and tenacity beyond belief.

When she came back to me in a level state of mind over the crack thing, the promise I had to make to her, in order for us to be able to work things out, was that I would stop using immediately and permanently. Of course, I made the promise. But also, of course, I broke it immediately. In fact, I had continued getting high the same night she had caught me in the act. After she left I felt terrible, ashamed, humiliated and afraid. But within an hour, I had to find a way to escape the reality of the situation, so I had driven back over to the 'hood, picked up another stem, copped another 50, and returned back home to get lost in my high again.

Back to the current situation, we pulled into her condo parking spot, got out, and went into her place without saying a word. The air was heavy, and I was getting nervous and anxious. We sat down on the couch together, and she asked me to put my hands in hers and look her straight in the eyes. Somehow, I managed to overcome my fear enough to do both. I looked at her, *really* looked at her, for the first time in a very long time. Aging has taken nothing away from her beauty, this fine African-American woman, with exotic facial features, high cheekbones, smooth dark brown skin, and a well-kept, short Afro that has recently begun to gray elegantly. She always dresses nice and carries herself with class and grace. Except, of course, when someone has incited her to anger, at which point she can go ballistic.

After a brief pause, in remembrance of her attractiveness, I am reminded of the potential danger I am in, and my mood returns to pensive, as she begins to speak. "Honey, you've got to promise me that you will tell me the truth. Do not lie to me, because I will know if you are. Do not treat me like I'm stupid, Marvin. I already know the answer to the question I'm going to ask you, and if you lie to me, I will know you are lying, and I will not be able or willing to try and forgive you, and work on getting back together with you, any longer. Look at me and promise me that you will be honest with yourself and me. Do you promise?"

I said, "Yes."

She then asked the most dreaded and unwelcome question that I had ever been not ready to face, or answer truthfully, in my entire life: "Marvin, are you using?" I started to formulate an answer, trying to dig up something to say that would not divulge the real truth, but she interrupted my hesitation with, "Don't lie to me, Marvin. I already know you are using. *Tell me the truth* … ***admit it!***

I said, "How do you *know* that? What kind of evidence do you have?" She replied, "I don't *need* any proof or evidence. I ***know*** you are. Now admit it, honey, *tell me the truth, are you still using crack?"*

I knew I was caught. There was no fooling her or myself

anymore, this was it, the dreaded moment of truth had finally arrived, and to lie was to lose every bit of redeeming value I might have left in my poor lost soul, so, after a long hesitation, I finally said, "Yes, I'm still using. I thought I could quit and keep my promise to you when I made it, but it's out of control, and I'm addicted to the stuff; and I'm so sorry, baby, I'm so sorry."

She then opened up her arms to me, I laid my head against her breast, and she held me as I wept, stroking my head and hair, and trying to console me that it was OK, the important thing was that I had had the courage to admit I had a problem. I was sobbing out of control, like a child who had been spanked for a wrongdoing and who also knew the spanking was well-deserved. I couldn't bear to look at her. I was so ashamed of what I had become and the pain, anxiety and disappointment I had brought upon her and my entire family, that I wished I could have crawled *under* a hole and disappeared.

After what seemed like an eternity, my crying subsided to the point where I could pause long enough to accept tissue papers and wipe my tears and blow my nose. I was shaking with grief and wishing I were dead. I managed somehow to pull up straight and look her once more in the eyes. I asked, "How did you know? How did you know for sure?"

She just smiled, sighed and replied that she and *all* the family had known for a long time, weeks in fact. My condition was so advanced that even the grandchildren had started asking, "What's wrong with Grandpa?" It was the strange and wild look in the eyes, the loss of skin color, the rapid weight loss, the desire to be alone all the time, the disappearing from family gatherings continuously, only to reappear with a different and unusual demeanor.

And of course, there was the fact that everyone knew I was earning nearly a thousand dollars a week as a carpenter, but

I was always broke, even to the point of asking family members, toward the end of almost every week, if they had a few bucks I could borrow until Friday, when I promised I could pay them back. Pretty simple, she said. They all knew I had a serious narcotics addiction; the only thing they did not know was if I was ever going to be man enough to admit it and try and get some help.

It all fell into place for me, and I began for the first time to see the transparency of my "secret life." I suddenly recalled, and related to my wife, the time about a week prior, when I had mistakenly dialed up my youngest brother on my cell phone. His speed dial on my phone was only one number different than the one I had designated for my dealer. I was high at the time and had inadvertently punched the wrong number. When he answered the phone, I was not cognizant of the fact that it was a family member on the line, and I started into my usual ghetto slang talk, about to set up a pickup, when I heard the other voice say, "Marvin, is that you?" I suddenly shook all over and felt a cold panic come over me. *Oh, God,* I thought, *It's my little brother!* My mind raced to try and remember what I had just said, what was I sounding like, how much I could have possibly divulged about my state of mind, and what amount of incriminating evidence I had revealed about my condition to this point.

It only took a split second to go through that thought process, and I quickly gathered myself, speaking intentionally slower, so I could concentrate on what I was actually saying and not slur my words. I laughed and put on a front, telling him I had dialed him up by mistake, and said something like, "but as long as I got you on the line, hey, how you doing, brother, long time no hear!" The conversation was brief, awkward, and ended with me feeling like an exposed fool who had just insulted my brother's intelligence. I had since forgotten all about it, of course, but he had not.

My brother is a Christian minister and a good one. He walks his talk and is in my estimation about the best example of a true Christian behaving as a real Christ you could ask for. His entire life and ministry are about loving and helping others, unconditionally and without judgment. He is also a "family-first" kind of guy who cares deeply about the wellbeing of the family as a whole and all the members of that family.

My wife told me, that very day he had phoned her to ask if everything was all right with me. She was glad to hear from him and had told him about her and the rest of the immediate family's fears, that I was addicted to crack. He had for some time been aware of, and concerned with, my excessive drinking, but this was too much for him to bear. He arranged to hold a family meeting between himself, my wife and my three children, and made the drive down to my wife's place immediately.

During the meeting, it was resolved that if my life were to be spared, it was going to have to be a proactive and group effort on their part, to intercede and *force* me, if necessary, to get help, even if it meant committing me to an institution for rehabilitation against my wishes. My son said, if necessary, he would hunt me down, knock me down, bind me, and physically carry me out to the car and drive me to the facility himself. No one at the table felt that I would be able to admit to myself and to them that I had a problem. They knew what a proud and arrogant person I was by nature, and they did not believe my ego would allow me to admit to my failure and lack of self-control over the situation.

No one believed I could do it, except for one: my wife.

She had asked the rest of the family to give her one last chance to try and talk to me before going to Plan B, which would be the forceful intervention. She told them she believed there was still a good man inside me somewhere, and she wanted the opportunity to give me a last chance to do the right thing and admit to her, without coercion, that I needed help. The rest of the family had begrudgingly agreed to this, and that was what (she explained to me as we were sitting on her couch together) had just happened. If I had not come clean and admitted to her that I had a problem just then, she had already agreed to slip out of my sight, make a phone call, and the rest of the family was poised to come over immediately. She was to stall me from leaving right away, long enough for them to get there, and they were all going to see to it that the next and *only* place I was going from there was to a rehabilitation facility.

Fortunately for me, I had passed the test. She told me how proud of me she was that I was man enough to admit I had a problem. Now, what was I going to do about it? I expressed that I sincerely wanted, and needed, professional help. I couldn't stand myself in this condition, and my life was nothing more than a horrible nightmare the way it was. I said as soon as a suitable place could be found for me to begin the rehabilitation process, I would go without delay, even if it were tomorrow morning.

In the meantime, I said I would work as fast as possible to finish the job I was on and save the money to go toward the rehab costs. I spent that entire evening with her without getting high.

I had so much crack in my system, she commented on the odd smell that was emanating from me. That night was the first, in a long time, that I actually got a full night's sleep. She did not sleep well because of all the twitching, grinding of the teeth, tossing and turning, and cold-sweat spells I was going through. Waking in the morning to a pillow soaked through and reeking with crack-saturated sweat, I groaned and moaned out loud. She asked what was wrong. I told her that although I meant every word I had said about ending this horrible habit (and I *did* mean it this time), I was afraid and scared to get out of bed and face the day.

We talked for a bit, and she said she felt it would be best, until a suitable rehab facility could be located, that I stayed with her. I agreed. At least from early evening to early morning, I would be in a safe and monitored environment with a loved one and out of temptation's way. I promised I would do my best to refrain from using during the day while at work. After breakfast, we both got in our cars and headed off in separate directions for our jobs. She told me she and our oldest daughter (who works at the same office as her) would be spending all their lunch and break times searching for a place for me to go and get well, and she assured me it would not take long to locate one.

I really *did* try to not use any crack that day. I tried harder than I ever had before, since the addiction had gotten control of me, that is. By noon, I was sweating and cold. I was feeling so disoriented, I was afraid to handle my power tools. The sounds they made pierced my ears and sounded surreal. My hands were shaking so bad, I feared I might wind up having an accident and cutting my fingers off. I went to a nearby party store and bought a half-pint of vodka and drank it down. That seemed to calm me down and ease the cravings a bit, and I went back to work. Then, around 2:30, a loud and authoritative voice boomed in my head with the command,

"YOU NEED ME RIGHT NOW. COME AND GET ME IMMEDIATELY!"

I know that must sound stupid and trite to anyone who has never had a serious narcotics addiction, but that is exactly the experience I had, and I'll bet you 10 to one that anyone reading this who has ever been a crackhead like me and tried to quit can verify that the drug actually *speaks* to you like the voice of God Himself. And I obeyed. I dropped everything, got in my car, and headed straight away to the 'hood, calling my dealer on the way.

I copped a 50, smoked most of it, felt wonderful again

for a while, and then I realized that I was not going to be able to keep this high going if I was to keep the promise to my wife and myself. I had to go home (her place) and face her within a few hours, and I dreaded the encounter. On the way back from work, I stopped at a favorite spot near her condo, lit up one last time for the day, smoked a cigarette to try and cover up the smell, pulled into the parking lot, got out, and nervously went up and rang the doorbell.

She knew right away I had used, of course. I denied it for a few minutes but soon gave in and told her the truth. She deserved the truth from me no matter how humiliated and worthless it made me feel. I owed her that, and much, much more, to say the least.

I told her I was sorry, I knew I had let her down, but this thing was so powerful, I really could not make it through a whole day on the job without using at least enough dope to not be going through the withdrawal symptoms. Withdrawal from crack is not nearly as *physical* as heroin withdrawal (I've read), it is more of a mental addiction, but it *is very real*, and I was unable to function all day without having at least some of it in my system. She forgave me, told me to keep on trying and fighting, do the best I could, and soon we would have a place where I could go and face the demon head on, without having to deal with "normal life" activities.

Days went by, and the search continued, but hope was diminishing with regard to finding a place we could afford. My daily usage was starting to creep back up again, and occasionally I would come home quite high, and my wife would explode in anger and frustration that I was not able to exercise *any* control over my habit. She had gone so far as to tell me that using a small mid-day dose to just get "straight" she could try and accept (for now, that is), and even allowed me to bring some vodka home at night, so I could appease my need to get high with liquor, which was a compromise of sorts; it was not nearly the high I craved but better than nothing for me, and the (*somewhat* comforting) feeling that I was at least using the lesser of two evils, for her.

We went on like this for a couple of weeks. The search for an affordable place that offered the entire necessary program, including detoxification, replenishing of nutrients, healthy diet, exercise, sauna sessions, individual psychotherapy, support groups, etc., was proving to be futile for anyone in my financial condition, and no one in the family had the funds to loan me, either. I was getting desperate, and so was my family. I feared I might lose it very soon and wind up giving up and going off on another binge, and so did they.

The only place we could find that provided at least *some* help was a three-to-five-day detoxification clinic located within the city. I agreed to go, even though I suspected this was going to be a far cry from the total healing process I really needed to undertake. Still, it was better than nothing. After about a two-day stint on the waiting list, I got the call from the clinic that they had a bed open. With my entire immediate family accompanying me, I went down and committed myself, taking finally the first step toward rehabilitation.

I was humbled and ashamed, but somewhere deep inside, I was a little bit happy with myself also for willingly taking this first actual initiative. I had been drinking heavily that day, to ward off the shakes, depression and anxiety I got from crack withdrawal, and as if to punctuate the immediate and pressing need for my treatment, when the intake counselor asked me to take a seat and answer some questions for the paperwork, I missed the chair completely and fell flat on my butt! A fitting embarrassment, and an exclamation point, to the dire straits I was in.

The detox clinic experience proved to be less than worthwhile. Yes, for three whole days I didn't have any crack or alcohol; in fact, they only served decaffeinated coffee, and no soft drinks containing caffeine were allowed, either. And, yes, I was thinking much more clearly and feeling a lot better after three entire days of complete abstinence from any mood-altering substances, eating regularly, and getting full nights' sleep. I got straight enough to give lip service to being reformed and felt ready to leave the facility. In truth, once I had regained mental stability, I was about to be driven mad in this environment.

All the other clients were repeat offenders, most having relapsed multiple times. The most prevalent topic of conversation was a sort of bragging session about how awful their lives had been due to their drug usage, with each trying to outdo the other's stories about how many drugs they had done and what amount of crazy and stupid acts they had performed under the influence of drugs and/or alcohol.

Having done the research, I knew what a real detoxification process for a crack addict consisted of, and nothing of that sort of regimen was provided. No vitamins, no nutritional supplements, no exercise programs (and no places or equipment where and with which to do your own exercise) were available. They had no sauna to sweat out the crack-laden fat cells, and the food was of average-to-poor quality. All this, of course, was not the well-intentioned staff's fault; there simply was not enough budget money available to provide these things for us "bottom-feeder" addicts.

Therapy consisted of group "12-step" in-house meetings, and we were required to attend AA meetings. Twice a day, all the patients were loaded into the "Druggie-Buggy" and shipped off to a local meeting of Alcoholics Anonymous. I found those meetings to be discouraging, demeaning and reprehensible. *No one* is told to ever consider his or her self cured … *EVER!* Once an addict, always an addict, that's their philosophy, and the "successful" members, the "winners" (they call them), are rewarded with a life of self-admission of total inability to heal himself or herself completely. They must introduce themselves in front of the group as alcoholics and/or addicts forever.

I witnessed on one occasion a certain elderly man stand up in front of the group. He had been sober for more than 30 years, and yet he introduced himself by saying, "Hi, my name is Bob, and I'm an alcoholic!" "Hi, Bob," the whole group said in unison, like an assemblage of robots programmed with a push-button-knee-jerk response. These people had all been brainwashed into the belief that they had *no hope of ever being free* of their addiction, there was *no cure* for them, and the only way they could control their addiction was to admit to their *utter powerlessness*. Keep going to the meetings, gut it out with total and grueling abstinence through each and every day, hour, and minute for the rest of your living days, get hooked up with a sponsor (one of the "winners"), and although *you will never be free of your addiction*, you just possibly may wind up being one of the lucky 16 percent who actually never relapse as a result of this miraculous program.

Now I had read enough about rehabilitation to know that there are recent developments in treatment therapy that have completely debunked this kind of philosophy. There are several clinics in existence in this country that have proven that clients have a far greater chance of not relapsing if they are treated as having an illness or disease that can and *must* be cured in order for complete recovery to happen and last. Alcoholism and substance abuse are the *symptoms* of the problem, not the problem itself. One clinic that operates under this philosophy in Hawaii ("Passages"), boasts an *84 percent success rate* … a complete reversal of the 84 percent *failure* rate among 12-step AA members!

Of course, only the well-to-do can afford to attend facilities like Passages. You need tens of thousands of dollars to complete those programs. AA on the other hand, is provided free and supported with member donations. So as I found myself relegated to being a "12-stepper," most of whom smoked cigarettes heavily and drank volumes of caffeinated coffee and soft drinks daily, while boasting about what derelicts they had been and how glad they are to have been sober for so long, and what a struggle they face each and every day of their lives, I started feeling frustrated and angry.

I knew I had brought everything on myself, that I was responsible for winding up in a situation like this, because of my string of errors in judgment and actions; but I couldn't help feeling like I was being cheated. All the tax dollars I had paid as a productive citizen and business owner in the past, and the only program I can afford to go to is this pathetic excuse for rehabilitation? I had one individual session with a psychotherapist while in residence at the detox clinic. He came once a week to provide counseling for the clients. I asked him point blank if there was any hope of me ever being really cured of my addiction. He said emphatically, "No, we do not teach or expect a cure. And the faster you give up the idea of being cured, the better for your rehabilitation."

Well, that was quite enough for me. The center allowed you to stay for up to five days, but you were free to go after three. I phoned my wife and asked her to come and get me out. She did not want to, insisting that it would be better for me to stay the whole five days. I warned her that if she did not come get me right then, I would run; if I had to stay another day in that place, I would surely lose my mind. I felt like I was in an insane asylum and needed out ***NOW.*** I promised her I was feeling fine and could now stop using, while we continued searching for a sane environment for me to complete the rehab process.

She complied, with expressed reservation, and on the third evening after my admission, I was never happier to see her car pull up in the drive. I grabbed my bags, said goodbye to a couple of friends I had made, wishing them well (and feeling sorry for them inside, for having to stay there any longer), and went back to her place. No way was I even *approaching* being fully rehabilitated, I knew, but I was determined not to use crack or alcohol any more, and to stay sober until I could be admitted to a better facility. I had proven to myself that I could go three full days without using, and that was something I could use as a positive basis from which to build on, *right?*

I fell flat and relapsed almost immediately.

The second day home, my wife was gone to work. I was staying at her condo for the day, not feeling ready to face the job environment just yet. My craving to get high started demanding my obedience. I walked to a party store about two miles away and purchased a half pint of vodka. I could have made a shorter walk to a closer party store, but that store was in the old 'hood, and I feared I might run into my dealer and be tempted to pick up some stone. I rationalized that a little liquor would be OK, once in a while. As long as I stayed off the crack I'd be fine, just until I could get some professional help.

But it didn't pan out that way. By the fourth day after leaving the clinic, I had returned to work. I had fibbed and told my employer before leaving I was going into the hospital for tests to see what was making me so tired and weak all the time, so my job was still waiting for me. Almost immediately, once I had gotten back out into "real world," the cravings began building up steam. Nothing so much physically, just strong messages coming from my brain that it would be all right to use some crack, it wouldn't hurt me. Then came messages in the form of *stronger* desire, and then *absolute necessity*. Sure enough, before the end of the afternoon, I had given into temptation, driven into the 'hood, copped a 50, bought a fresh stem and some char, and I fired up the rock once again. I actually told myself that it would only be this one time, "just for old times sake," and that I would resume abstinence again the next day.

Amazingly, that first evening after picking up again, my wife did not notice it. Perhaps she had her guard down and wasn't looking as hard for the signals. I don't know, but I was relieved, to say the least. However, within a week after the first pickup, I was a full blown addict again, copping and using every day; and within two weeks, my habit was right back up where it had left off before detox. My wife knew it, my kids knew it, and this time, although I tried to deny it for a short while, I knew it and admitted it, too. I had relapsed, I was a crackhead again, and I needed help desperately and immediately.

There was no help available. And this time, my wife was fed up. She had had it. She called me one morning while I was at work. I had shown up at her place the night before, blasted out of my mind on crack. She said she had packed my clothes and things in a couple of garbage bags and set them by the door. She ordered me to go over during the day, pick up my stuff, leave my keys on the coffee table, and get out. She did not want me to be there when she got home and never wanted to see me again in my condition as a crackhead, which was all the time.

She said she would pray for me and hoped I would eventually get my act together, but she was all through coddling me, she needed to get on with her life, and no way was she going to live another day with a drug addict for a roommate, let alone a husband. I tried to assure her that I was searching the Internet every day for a rehab clinic (which I was), and I promised to get help as soon as I could, but she was having nothing of it. "Don't come around me anymore unless and until you are rehabilitated, and good luck, because I don't believe anything you say any more, I don't believe you will ever be sober again, and I am through trying to help you" is what she was making clear to me. Furthermore, she informed me, I had lost my entire family, also. "Goodbye and good riddance" was the gist of the message.

The same day, my mother called me. She told me she had heard of a clinic on the other side of the state that took patients even if they had little or no money. It was a full yearlong program, complete with detox and therapy, and boasted an 80-plus percent rate of success. I was elated at the news and called my wife. She said she was glad to hear it, but she didn't believe I would really see it through to the end, and although she hoped to the contrary, she just couldn't believe any promises of mine. "Don't call me anymore, just go and do what you have to do, Marvin, and leave me out of your life." Before she hung up, I asked her to listen for just a second longer. I promised her that even though she didn't believe me, I would be finishing up the job I was on within a week, and I would take that money and finance my trip over to and entry into the rehab clinic. I heard an apathetic yawn, "Sure, whatever, OK," and she hung up.

I really *was* intending to turn myself in for help. And I was angered and frustrated that I was being kicked out of the house and abandoned, now that I had finally found a place where I believed I could get the help I needed. I went over to my wife's condo, picked up my bags, left the key to the door on the table, took one last long and wistful look at the soft and comfortable world I was now expelled from, closed the door behind me, and left.

Back in my car, I called the facility my mother had recommended to me and talked with an intake counselor. Within a few minutes, I was disillusioned and desperately frustrated. This facility was a fundamentalist, rightwing, Bible-thumping charismatic Christian organization, that ran a strict, rigorous and arduous daily schedule, with little or no personal freedoms, and certainly no religious freedom of thought. The daily schedule consisted of Bible study, prayer meetings, group testimonials, chapel meetings, and afternoon labor sessions, and the evenings were full of more of the same. When asked if they had psychotherapy as part of their treatment, he replied that they had Christian counselors who helped their patients to see through their sinful ways, repent, and find Jesus.

Well, this is just great, I thought. I finally find a place I can afford, and it's basically a Christian monastic boot camp. Church time, 24/7. I told him that I had my own spiritual path already. He had the audacity to ask me if I had considered how good a path it was if I had wound up an addict. I sniped back combatively that I supposed there had *never* been *any Christian addicts* show up at their door before, *had there?* And where had *their* paths gotten *them?* Clearly this was not the ideal place for me. Even as a crackhead I was ready to take up arms against religious stupidity. However, I knew I was on a death path for sure in the state I was in. It was a Thursday, and I committed to myself that if by Friday of the next week, I had not found any better place to go, I would submit myself to this torture, it being the lesser of two evils when placed alongside my current situation.

Part Three: The Last Curtain Call

But in the meantime, I resolved I was going to have one last "Hurrah!" I was determined to have one final blowout weekend of devil-may-care fun. One last binge, one last adventure into the depths of debauchery, before turning myself in. I went to my client's home, collected a draw on my work, cashed the check, and headed for the 'hood with $1,500 cash in my pocket. I copped an eight ball, loaded up, and started *lettin'er rip.*

A couple of hours into the binge, my phone rang. *It was my mother.* She said, **"Marvin, the Devil is making a play for your soul."** I shook all over. I couldn't talk to her. I knew she was right, but I didn't want to hear it right then and got her off the phone as quick as possible. I got higher. My phone rang again. *It was my youngest daughter*. She was practically screaming at me, telling me that if I wouldn't turn myself in right then, that day, she would drive up and down the streets of the areas I was haunting, find me, and have the cops help her if necessary to bring me in and have me committed. I promised her I would go in on Monday. She pled with me, reminding me that I might not even *live* that long in the state I was in. She offered to let me come over and stay with her until I could get admitted. She knew her mother had kicked me out, and I was living in the streets, basically, because I had lost the other place where I used to stay.

I paused for a moment. I looked at the only partially used large eight ball, and (the addict in me) told her I just couldn't stay with her for the weekend, but I would be OK, and I would keep my promise to start the intake procedure on Monday morning. She ended the conversation with a reminder that her door was always open, and she would be elated if I showed up at any time before Monday, she was so worried for me.

The next 36 hours were a blur of wild and bizarre states of mind and reckless behavior. I went through nearly $600 worth of crack. I scored a couple of tabs of ecstasy with the full intention of picking up a girl, dropping the hits together with her, and having some out-of-my-mind sex. That never happened (the sex, that is); at least I'm pretty sure it didn't. I think I must have gotten too high to remember my intentions, and I don't remember *everything* I did that night, even to this day. I *do* remember I went to lots of clubs, scored stone after stone, smoking and drinking endlessly. Around midnight, with a couple drinks and the promise of getting her high, I hooked up with another prostitute I had met a couple days before. A Hispanic girl, a little pudgy, short, not very good looking in the daylight, but fine enough for me then, in the state of mindlessness I was in.

She had finished her business for the night and was ready to party. I had cash and stone, and she had connections, if we needed more of anything. It was fun to have a friend (of sorts) to share my carousing with, another crackhead companion, who shared the same lust for insanity as I had. We talked, laughed, drank, went out repeatedly to the car to hit the rock, came back in and danced and partied hearty, staying until they closed down the bar. Then we went to her place and whiled away the early Saturday morning hours, using up the last bag of stone I had with me. She invited me to spend the night there, telling me to go lie in her bed. She said she'd be in there in a minute to give me some oral sex and told me I could sleep in as long as I wanted. I lay down and passed out before knowing if she ever came into the room. I remember it was 6:30 in the morning.

The next thing I knew, I was outside in my car, somewhere in some neighborhood I didn't recognize. The car was parked, with the motor running. I was in the back seat, fully dressed, with my jacket and someone else's cap on. Groggy and fuzzy, I searched my brain for answers as to who and what and where I was. I started coming to my senses, realizing I was probably in harm's way. I felt panicky and started searching my person for anything missing. I discovered I had been robbed of my cell phone and about five hundred dollars. I felt a bruise on top of my head, touched it, and saw blood on my fingers. In terror, it suddenly occurred to me that I'd better get out of there; for all I knew, whoever had driven me this far might be planning to come back, kill me, and steal the car, too.

I jumped into the driver's seat and pulled out as fast as I could. My head was throbbing and felt as heavy as the world, and I was having trouble focusing my eyes. Fortunately, my robber had overlooked the $100 bill I had tucked under the driver's seat in an old envelope. I thought for a moment about scoring another stone. Right then, a voice inside me said, with absolute authority, ***"No, Marvin, this is the end of this road. Go to your daughter's house and turn yourself in. Do it now and don't turn back."***

And so it was, at 8:00 a.m., Saturday morning, November 12, 2005, my days of living the life of a crack addict came to an end. I pulled my car into the parking lot of my daughter's apartment. I walked through the patio door, which they always leave open when someone is home. I walked into the kitchen, where my son-in-law was preparing breakfast for the boys, sat down at the kitchen table, and said to him, "It's over, man … I'm all done." He didn't say a word, just nodded knowingly at me. He then told me to make myself comfortable, his wife would be home later, and I would be safe and welcome here for as long as I needed to stay. I went over to the couch, and with tears in my eyes, lay down. Twitching and shaking all over, I struggled to relax, but eventually I felt a sense of relief, then a collapsing feeling, and finally I passed out of consciousness.

The rest of the morning and afternoon, I was in and out of consciousness. I remember my son-in-law bringing me some food, and thankfully eating it. I remember my daughter coming home. She hugged and kissed me, and thanked me for doing the right thing, saying she was glad I was here and relieved to know I was still alive and OK. Everything was going to be all right, she assured me. I handed her my remaining money, the keys to my car, and my cell phone. (I had had two of them, and this one had not been stolen). That way I knew I could not get into any more trouble and was powerless to leave, go anywhere, buy anything, or do anything stupid, before getting some help. Then I went back to sleep.

Several hours later, I awoke to a nudging from someone. I struggled through my hazy eyes to focus and see who it was. As if in a vision, I saw three angels hovering over me; and then, within a second or two, they were revealed to me again as my beloved children, all three of them, standing over me, alongside the couch. "Get up, Dad," my youngest daughter said. "We're taking you to the ER for a checkup and detox." I did so, willingly and thankfully. My wife joined us all at the hospital. I was given some tests and pronounced healthy enough to be discharged.

Soon after leaving the hospital, my wife drove me

halfway to the city where my younger brother lived. The plan had already been made for me. He was on his way to meet us. We were to rendezvous at a certain exit, I was to be transferred into his car and go back with him to his home, where I would be safe to begin my detoxification and rehabilitation, under his and his wife's care, until I could gain admission into a suitable facility; that being, most probably, the Christian program I described in detail earlier.

The bad dream was about to end. I was waking up. And I was terrified. Was I going to leave one nightmare only to end up in another?

CHAPTER TEN

THE ROAD TO RECOVERY

My wife pulled into the designated gas station parking lot, and before long, here came my brother. I was still so saturated with residual cocaine in my system that I was barely coherent half the time, feeling dizzy and fuzzy, twitching, sweating and feeling cold, all at the same time. Still, I was overjoyed to see him, and we shared a big hug, and he and my wife shared the same. After a brief interchange of pleasantries and loading my bags into his car, I turned to say goodbye to my wife.

It's not even funny how life can break you down and humble you. I've never been a stoic and have always been capable of shedding occasional tears of sorrow or joy, but the past six months had turned me into a complete emotional slob by this time. As I gazed into her fearful and anxious eyes, those eyes that were my open portals into the depths of her sweet soul and the loving, caring heart of compassion and forgiveness she carries within her breast, I just couldn't stand it. I wept as we hugged and said our goodbyes.

She was crying also but had the strength to gather herself and impart some of that strength into me, assuring me that I was going to be fine; she knew, and was comforted, that I would be safe now. She told me she had restored faith in me, that I would make it through to a complete healing and would be able to return to her one day as a whole man again. I kissed her long and deeply, gave her one last squeeze, and promised that one day I *would* return to her and be the husband she deserved and the father and grandfather our kids and grandkids needed to be able to look up to again. Promising to come visit me soon, she drove off, and I stood and stared in her direction long after she had passed out of my sight.

All of her assurances received notwithstanding, I was literally shaking throughout my heart, body and soul with the fear and anxiety of what lay ahead for me. This was to be the biggest battle of my life, I knew, and it *was a matter of life and death.* My brother kept me entertained with light-hearted talk all the way to his house. I suspect he knew that providing diversion through conversation would keep my mind off the dreaded gravity of the situation and the resulting self-defeating inner dialogue that was beating the life (and nearly all the will to live) out of me. But there *was* a small glowing ember that I felt beginning to warm my cold shivering heart. *I had made the move.* And as we drove along the highway, I felt a strange and comforting feeling of peace begin to well up in me.

I recognized that this highway I was traversing with my brother was my road to recovery. Yet I had no idea, at the time, where I was really going to wind up. The idea that I would most probably have to face a year of being force-fed fundamentalist Christianity, in a strict environment of isolation with religious zealots, was nearly as brutal a thought as returning to the pipe. I feared I would end up fleeing before I could be healed. But I had made a promise and meant to keep it. Maybe I could gut it out at least long enough to get really clean and healthy; fake my way through all the chapel meetings, prayer meetings, altar calls, testimonials, etc., long enough to feel strong and sound before taking flight.

I knew how to do all that phony religious stuff from my childhood and young adult years. I would just play the game, tell everybody I had gotten saved (thanks *so much* to them), and if they were the same typically simple-minded Christians I had long stereotyped, I could easily push all the right buttons and they'd be satisfied I was "one of them" now, so they would all feel better about themselves and leave me alone to my private thoughts. I would keep an inner sanctum where the truth resided, where I was still a free spirit and an independent thinker. There was only one problem with this plan, and I knew it could prove to be a fatal one. It would mean I would have to keep on living a lie.

Living a life of lies had been hard enough when I had a place of my own, where I could retreat from those I had to lie to. How was I going to keep up *this* proposed charade when I would be living in an open room dormitory of bunk beds, constantly monitored by staff counselors? Worse yet, though I am no psychotherapist, I knew in my heart and mind that the healing and curing process could not possibly be 100 percent successful long-term if I didn't learn how to *stop* living behind a shield of lies!

With these types of thoughts, schemes and fears going around and around in my fuzzy cracked-up head, we finally arrived at my brother's house. I was so weary, burned out, ashamed, depressed and clouded with lingering narcotics coursing through my tired body and mind, I really can't remember much about the rest of that evening. As I write this sentence, I have been clean and sober for well over two months, and my memory banks still come up blank when asked to recall any vivid memories of distinct events during that time. All I remember, vaguely, was warm greetings, hugs, a sense of assurance and love from everyone in the house, and taking welcome refuge in the warm bed and private room they provided me. I suspect everyone was glad to see me go to bed and get some much-needed sleep, because I am most certain my physical appearance, sullen demeanor, defeated psyche, and crushed soul cast a weight into the air that would be difficult for anyone to bear for long.

I don't know how long I slept or what time it was I got up the next day, but I did feel a little better. I resolved to enjoy the day as much as I could and every day I had left before being committed to the religious boot camp. My head was still quite fuzzy, and my mind was *screaming* at me for drugs, *outraged* that I had put myself in this position where I could not obey its mental orders to get high. I got out of bed and dressed, and started looking around the house, getting my bearings, ready to make anything I could out of the day.

It must have been early, because no one was up and moving about yet, so I wound up sitting in the kitchen in the breakfast nook, staring out the window, lost in my private musings. Then I heard a rustling upstairs and then footsteps coming down the stairs, and that's when I met my sister-in-law. I will call her Theresa for the purposes of my story.

I had seen Theresa a few times before at family gatherings and talked with her briefly over the phone now and again, but I had never spent any time with her and never had a conversation of any length or depth enough to learn much of anything about her or what she was really like. To me, she had always just been my little brother's wife, and I assumed she was just another typical good-hearted, well-intentioned Christian lady, a church-going religious person, who had nothing much to say or offer, other than quoting the scriptures.

I've always thought of it as the "Christian Virtue of Plagiarism of Wisdom." You know, memorize the Bible, learn how to connect the scriptures to each and every life situation you face, and then you can feel (and give the impression of being) enlightened because you always have the right thing to say and wise advice to give, without having to do any thinking for yourself. I had no reason to respect or disrespect Theresa as a person, however, since, as I said, I had never *really* met *with* her, and as my relative-in-law I was ready to find out a lot more about her, with as much of an open mind as I could muster.

Boy, was I in for a big surprise. Within minutes, after she had sat down across from me, looked me deep in the eyes, paused for a moment, and then began talking with me, I knew I was sitting and conversing with someone very special, someone with a great deal of sagacity and insight. This was no typical (to me at the time) Christian religious nut. This was as *real* person. I quickly started to like her. We must have talked for an hour, at least. I didn't know it at the time, but Theresa was already starting my therapy and laying the groundwork and ground rules for a healing process that had not yet become obvious to me. She's a clever and sly gal, with lots of skillful means about her, I now know.

Within a couple of days, I was feeling much better. I could think more clearly again, and my body was thanking me for the much-needed replenishing of food and nutrients it was getting. I was eating like a horse after a race, several times a day. My mind, of course, was still *enraged* with the whole situation and continued savagely with its onslaught against my will and feelings of self-worth. I felt like a murderer that was cursed with a conscience, sentenced to living in a halfway house with the relatives of his victim. Not *all* the time did I feel this way, of course, and with each day, the episodes would come less often and last not as long, but I was still often enough depressed, sometimes suicidal.

By the end of the first week, with continuous love and genuine concern for me, expressed through words and touch by everyone around, I had garnered some strength and was feeling halfway decent about facing each new day when I awoke. I was even having occasional extended periods of actually feeling good, and my old mistress and mental slave master had pretty much given up on the idea that I was going to listen to her commanding tirades and bolt back to the slave's quarters, where she could beat me and whip me, and then reward me with some more of her magical pig slop. I hated her now, hated her enough to *kill* her for what she had done to my life and me. Yet the diminishing part of me that still *was* her remained alive inside me, and I often trembled at the thought that she could rise to power again, if I were not completely victorious in this battle; taking no prisoners, slaughtering every last vestige of even the most remotely tenable "thought servants" of hers within my mind.

Nothing much was being said to me about when I would be shipped off to the monastery, and I had pretty much given up on any hope of alternatives for my long-term rehabilitation, so I just tried to live each day to its fullest and enjoy the non-judgmental and unconditional love Theresa and everyone in the house was bestowing upon me. She would often talk with me for long periods and would tenderly probe my bruised psyche with soft but firm and healing queries into my life, my past, and how I felt about then and now, what did I think was the root cause of my downfall, etc.

She made me feel so welcome and appreciated *just as I was,* even in this lowly condition, that I felt I could genuinely trust her; and I opened up deep inner parts of me that I hadn't even dared to face or deal with *myself* in many, many years. I could use my swear words in front of her, tell her the most shameful and sinful acts I had committed, and she was not phased, or dissuaded from me, in the least. She even expressed that she saw so many wonderful qualities in me, she felt thankful for the opportunity to get to know me and was gaining much value herself from our conversations.

By the end of that first week, we also developed such a mutual trust, she even opened up to *me* and told me about things, deeds, habits, tendencies and challenges in her past that had forged her into what she was today. This was no typical, sheltered little pushover "goody-two-shoes" kind of Christian; this was a woman who had been around the block *several* times and back, had survived to talk about it, and was able to use her worldly experiences and the attendant wisdom gained to relate to me in a way I needed most. She was single-handedly destroying many of my long-held and sacred religious prejudices, by her very existence and example.

That first full weekend of my stay, my wife came to visit me and stayed for a couple of days. She was glad to see me looking so well, with the color coming back to my skin, my eyes looking clear again, and I had even put a few pounds on, looking far less emaciated than the ghost she had dropped off at the gas station a week earlier. We spent some much-needed time together and were given the freedom to come and go as we pleased, even spending the night at a motel in town. Theresa and my brother invited us to attend their church service, and although as I have explained earlier, I have never been much of a church lover, something told me to go. I heard that familiar little voice tell me that, knowing what I did of my sister-in-law and brother, this just might be a valuable experience, and certainly I owed it to them to show up and see what their ministry was all about, firsthand. My wife agreed, and we got dressed that Sunday morning and headed off to church.

My idea about church was about to be changed forever. As an old hippie, I've always felt "the vibes, man," and the vibes in the house were sky high with love, fun and good feelings. They held their services in an old Moose Lodge, a bar, basically. There was nutritious hot food to eat, beat music going on, spirited conversations, kids running all over the place, wild-haired teenagers with body piercings, tattoos and sagged pants, receiving and giving hugs, and love, with stodgy looking older folks (like me), and it was just like a good old party goin'on! They weren't serving any alcohol, and if you wanted to smoke you had to go outside, but even if you *had* been drinking, or *even getting high* the night before, you were welcome here. There were people of all ages, races, education and economic levels, and social backgrounds all enjoying each other's company, laughing, joking, having great fun together.

When the "service" started, it was highly spirited music for at least an hour. People clapped, sang, danced, let loose, and expressed their selves openly, spontaneously and unashamedly. There was a freedom here that harked back to the "good old days" when hippies tried their best to free up the stoic Christians of the times with the Jesus Freak Movement. Here it was, right now, in full view, a real spiritual happening, *Christianity finally being done right*, and I was impressed and happy beyond belief. My wife and I sang, clapped our hands, and boogied along, enjoying every moment.

Once the crowd had spent itself of any and all excess kinetic energy, my brother and pastor of the congregation launched into his message for the day. Already my preconceptions about any and all Christian churches had been smashed to smithereens, and he was just then getting ready (I now know) to smash the insides out of me and reduce me to a pulp.

He talked about God's Grace: the unconditional, unchanging, nonjudgmental, uncompromising gift of forgiveness and acceptance from God that was *free for anyone* who would accept the offer. The entire service I was bucking internally, fighting my guts.I wasn't ready to hear or accept this. No way could anything be so easy and still true. I was a bad person who had committed travesties against myself and everyone who cared about me. I was a drug addict. I was a liar. I was a cheat. I was a sexual and ethical whore. No way, brother, good try, dog, but I ain't buyin' it. I need psychotherapy for my healing, not some Grace from God … doesn't apply to, or work, for me, sorry, Bucko.

But he was relentless.

He went on, and on, and on about the healing power of grace and told true stories of people who had been worse than even me, who had been made whole and reversed their ways of error and sin in an instant of acceptance. I was sweating, feeling feverish, and trembling. My brother asked the congregation to stand, as he prayed for those in need of grace in the room. Somehow I managed to get up. Then I had an experience I'll never be able to aptly communicate in words, because it was truly spiritual. It would be best described as a feeling that a gentle warm hand descended upon me and laid its palm on top of my head and stroked my forehead with its fingers. I calmed down physically, right away. It then proceeded to drift through my skull and sank into my brain. My mental state became calm and open.

Then this hand drifted down into my chest and massaged my heart, holding it for a moment that seemed eternal. I heard a voice say, **"You are loved by me, and accepted by me, and I want nothing more than for you to be with me, forever."** I was not much more than a puddle by now, tears pouring down my cheeks, and struggling to remain standing. Within a few short seconds that had seemed like several hours while it was happening, I was set free by this miraculous power of Grace. I was forgiven, healed, and relieved of the awful and frightful responsibility of carrying my guilt around, as though it represented *me* any more.

Now I just had to forgive *myself*. That's a lot harder; more on that later.

After the service, my wife and I went back to the house together, and on the way we spoke at length in the car about what was next for me and us. She reaffirmed my belief (by now) that the possibility of finding and funding a suitable clinic for my extended rehab was out of the question, at least for the immediate future. I told her how strongly I felt about the progress I had made at the house this past week, how that, together with today's healing experience, was compelling me to ask my brother and sister-in-law if it would be at all possible to extend my stay. We talked for some time about it and finally agreed that if it were acceptable to them, here would be the best place available for me to continue to rehabilitate.

When brother and sister-in-law got home, we sat together to talk. I told them of my experience at the service, and both were overjoyed. I expressed that I felt like a wayward traveler who had been wandering about for years, lost and without a map, and that I felt I had finally made it home, weary and exhausted, from the long and grueling journey. After a bit, I got up the nerve to ask them if I could stay on longer, at least for a while. Almost immediately, Theresa spoke for the both of them and said, "Marvin, you can stay here for as long as you want or need to. Our home is open to you, and you are welcome to be here with us."

What a relief! What joy! We talked for a time longer and set about putting our heads together on how all the necessary elements for successful rehab could be accomplished within this environment. Good nutritious food was no problem, and my wife committed herself and the rest of the immediate family to contributing to the budget as much as possible, to help compensate for the cost of my ravenous appetite. Vitamins and nutritional supplements were available. Exercise and sauna could be obtained, through an inexpensive membership at the local YMCA, and I could ride with any of the family house members since they all went there regularly anyway.

I didn't know it at the time, but shortly after that meeting, even the need for professional counseling was available "in-house," because Theresa was a degreed therapist and counselor. My wife and I had expressed to her that I needed to find a local professional to help with that part of my recovery, and that's when she divulged her professional credentials *and willingness* to fulfill that particular need. *That sly little stinker,* I thought to myself when I heard the good news. She had been *treating* me all along, and in an instant, a lot of things fell into place in my mind, as I re-ran the "conversations" we had been having back in my head. She had artfully and skillfully brought me to a place in my heart and mind wherein I could receive the message my brother had delivered that Sunday in church. Needless to say, I was hardly upset by being "duped" or "led down the primrose path" by this godly tag team; I was grateful and appreciative beyond measure.

So it came to pass that the "Shiloh's Lighthouse Ministries" opened up a new branch of operations, through their organic, freewheeling Christian style of spiritual outreach and founded what I will call for the rest of my story, "Camp Shiloh." I was the first, and only patient, at the time, and I was easily heads and shoulders above *any* of the other clients with regard to progress made thus far. And the progress would continue on successfully, I knew, because I was grounded now, healed with grace, and ready to dig deeper into this guy called "Marvin" with Theresa's help; here within the comforting confines of Camp Shiloh.

CHAPTER ELEVEN

PATIENCE

Due to my new-found spiritually invigorated attitude and zeal for total healing and rehabilitation, coupled with Theresa's adeptness and heart of compassion, I became a quick study and made remarkable progress. I was able to cry less often and regressed rarely into the periods of depression and thoughts of self-condemnation that had been so frequent earlier. I was able to laugh again, even laugh at myself, which she pointed out, and I agreed, was a *good* thing. It was nothing short of an abbreviated miracle, when compared to the seemingly eternal and complicated professional programs I had read about that cost a wealthy man's inheritance to afford. One day for a lark, I wrote the spoof recreated for you here: it is funny in part, because of its representation of a true happening.

Camp Shiloh's 90-Day Drug Abuse Rehab Program

Week One: Client is allowed to rest, eat anything he/she wants, as often as he/she wants. No responsibilities are given to the client, just hug him/her a lot and say kind things about what a fine person he/she is, how so many family and friends are pulling for him/her, and how God is working a miracle in his/her life.

Week Two: If the client insists, begrudgingly allow him or her to do some small tasks around the facility. Staff members must overcome their tendency to treat clients as guests and instead help them regain a sense of self-worth through (small steps at a time) manual labor and accomplishment of assignments.

Morning therapy sessions happen at random times and on random days. Emphasis is placed on personal self-discovery of what, and where, the inner pain is and where it has come from. Discussions about God, theology, the human condition, and man's meaning of life as it relates to the universe are essential at this point. The client is not force-fed any particular belief about God, Christianity, Jesus, Holy Trinity, etc., but staff continues to show by example what the true spirit of Christ-like living is all about. If client has any applicable skills, he/she is asked (but not forced) to perform, or help in anyway possible, with the ministry's Sunday Services.

If client is married, conjugal visits are now allowed, even encouraged, and client and spouse can leave the facility as they choose and return anytime they like.

Staff continues "hugs therapy" with client.

Weeks 3 & 4: Client by now is usually ready to be given mentoring assignments. In order for the client to fully understand the Biblical admonition that one should give in order to receive, he/she is given the outpatient assignment of mentoring one (or a few) young people who need a "Big Brother or Big Sister" in their life. This work is to be carried out alone by the client, with no staff supervision.

Therapy sessions and theological discussions continue, again with emphasis on client forming his/her own conclusions and no pressure put on him/her to believe any certain way or another. Work periods and "hugs therapy" continue as usual, and client has the option at all times of taking a nap or going for a walk just because he/she feels like it.

Weeks 5-8: Client is now ready to prepare for overseas missions work. In addition to the above ongoing curriculum, client is put in charge of raising several thousand dollars to fund a missions program, within three weeks. Client is instructed to not question if this is possible, but to trust in God and let Faith do its work. Client is given freedom to leave the facility at any time necessary, and go wherever necessary, to meet with possible donors, sell the vision and need for funding, collect the checks, and return to the facility all by his/her self.

The rest of the curriculum goes on as usual.

Month Three: Now a fully recovered ex-addict with a valuable story to tell and the ability to help with Shiloh's ministry, client is offered the opportunity to join staff on an overseas missions venture if he/she wishes. Upon return from this mission, he/she is offered a position on staff; again, with no pressure, but if God leads client in that direction, then so be it.

Sounds too good to be true, I know, but it really is not much of an exaggeration. Within weeks, I had gained confidence and resolve, was actively engaged in youth outreach programs, and was using my musical talents in the ministry's services. Everything was going smoothly. However, the one remaining obstacle for complete and total healing was my inability to be as forgiving of myself as God had been. Occasionally, I would reach an impasse in progress, because I would get so eager to be free to do all the things "normal" people do, and I had no means yet with which to do them.

By this I mean I would get jealous of others in the house who had their own transportation and could go when and where they pleased, without having to ask if they could go and do, and not have to borrow someone's car to do it. I wanted money in my pocket, my *own* money that I had *earned.* I wanted to have my cell phone back. I wanted to have my wife back and be able to support her and start repaying the immense debt of gratitude I owed her. I would regress when these feelings and desires came over me, into periods of frustration and feelings of low self-esteem, and withdraw from everyone into long walks by myself or solace within the quarters of my private room. And Theresa was always right there, in an instant, picking up on my defeatist thinking and emotions like a bloodhound in pursuit of a scared rabbit.

I remember one day, I had become jealous of her. She announced to me that she had made plans to go see my wife and spend a day or more with her, just to talk and see how she was doing, what she was feeling, etc., a "girls thing," you know. Now this was something I had long hoped for, them getting together, I had even *advocated* it, because I worried a lot and often about my wife and regularly daydreamed about how she was coping with her lonely life in her empty condo. Telephone conversations we had nearly every day, but nothing compares with *being with* the one you love. I knew that spending some time with Theresa, and getting some psychological help and friendly support, would be beneficial for her. Still, when Theresa said she was going, I was overcome with envy.

I seethed internally for a while and wallowed in thoughts of what a useless failure I was. How powerless was I and how completely and utterly dependent on others I remained, like some lazy welfare recipient. I bolted out of the house and went on a long, fast walk. I walked so hard, and so long, I was out of breath when I finally returned to the house. I didn't want to see or talk to anyone, I just wanted to get to my room and be left alone. Wasn't happening. Theresa was right there, the instant I got in the door. Like a laser-guided missile, she had sensed that something was amiss with me and had been asking everyone where I had gone during my walk. She was on me like white on rice, asking probing questions about how I was feeling, was there anything we needed to talk about, all the questions I wanted nothing of right then.

I somehow got her off my back by reassuring her with (the lies) that I was fine, just wanted some fresh air and exercise, hence my heavy breathing, and I retreated to my room. I was having serious thoughts of giving up on the idea of *ever* being able to be whole again. I was feeling disoriented and confused, and my old mistress and master was reminding me of what a pathetic waste I have always been, still was today, and she was causing me to remember how good she used to make me feel, whenever I got this despondent. Suddenly, I heard a "knock, knock" on my door. "Jesus Lord," I almost shouted out loud, "will this woman *ever* leave me alone?"

I answered the door, and sure enough, there was Theresa. She came in, sat down, and insisted that I level with her about what was going on in my mind. I was cornered like a wounded animal, and I finally broke down and confessed that I was indeed going through these feelings and was nearly at my wits end with frustration over my state of mind and sense of helplessness. Once again, she came through with just what I needed to hear.

She reminded me that I was less than two months into a rehabilitation process that often took six months to a year anywhere else I might have wound up. My success and progress to this point had been nothing short of incredible and were something to be proud of, she said, and of course she was right on. She pointed out to me that I was now my own worst remaining enemy, and she led me to understand that although I had received the divine gift of Grace, I was still bound by my own attachment to the past and how I *had* been, prior to the healing process. I was still carrying the baggage of guilt with me, and occasionally I would still stumble and fall under the weight, unless, and until, I was able to once and for all forgive myself completely and let go of this steaming pile of feces that was still stinking me up.

"Patience, Marvin," she said to me. "We all need to learn patience, and patience is the most important lesson for you right now." And I got it. She was right. Crackheads, and any other kind of addicts, have *no patience whatsoever*, and I had long ago lost any resemblance to the once tolerant, nearly imperturbable, person I had been years ago. She joked, "We all ask, 'God, please give me patience, and ***GIVE IT TO ME RIGHT NOW!'"*** I laughed, she laughed with me, we hugged long and sincerely, expressed our love for each other, and I was fine again. More importantly, I resolved, from that day forward, to remain centered within my mind whenever those impatient and self-defeating thoughts would pass through, and to forgive myself, as I had already been forgiven.

The next morning, I received a reaffirmation of my need to follow through with my new resolve by observing the housedog at Camp Shiloh, "Bow." Bow is a wonderful creature, and as most dogs do, he shows his emotions, desires and feelings freely and openly. He has no self-consciousness and cares nothing in the least what others think of him. If he is hungry, or wants to play, or wants a treat, or wants to go outside, he'll let you know about it. And he has no patience whatsoever. He will run about, squeal, yelp, and put on a fitful display of lack of self-control, if he does not get his way *immediately.* "Good and fine enough for lovable Bow, but no more dog-like behavior for me," I thought.

CHAPTER TWELVE

THE WORK AHEAD

Less than 10 weeks ago, as I sit here at my computer writing, I had my work with me, and I had my work ahead of me. That's what crack addicts call their drug of choice and all the paraphernalia that goes with usage, saying things like, "Got any work, player? Need some work, dog? Yo, where can I score some work?" My work was my life, my only reason for living, and I was dying in the process. My work was everything to me, and I put everything I had into my work.

I now have some new work. This new work is everything to me now, and I will put everything I am, and have, into it. It is divinely inspired work that now drives me and propels me into a "Brave New World" each and every day I am blessed with another sunrise, another opportunity to witness to the world and help others, in any way I can, to be thankful: thankful for the talents and spiritual gifts they have, not the least of which is their very own precious gift of life, and free will. I have learned the hard way about the perils of self-centeredness, and pointless whining, and despair, over what I do not have. I have stopped pining over what I shall eat, or what I shall wear, or what I shall earn, and have to keep.

I could die right now and be happy. Whether or not I ever again earn a single penny, own another possession, or receive another blessing in any form whatsoever, sufficient for a lifetime is this moment of unmitigated rapture and peace. I have lived through the cold winter of the soul, survived the realms of Hell and the onslaught of the Hungry Ghosts. Through the Grace of God, I have been given new life, the opportunity to see yet another dawn, and now am surrounded by the Holy Ghost.

My journey has come full circle, and I am home. The wayward Prodigal Son has returned to his father, and there is a celebration going on. As I recall the travels and lessons learned, I can see now, how each step of the way, each phase of discovery was a carefully laid-out plan to lead me to the place where I could connect with God, in my own way, in my own time. I would not recommend my path of learning to anyone faint of heart and sometimes consider it scarcely believable that I am still alive and of sound body and mind today.

My mind is once more clear and focused enough to resume the deep meditations that I had let go of years ago. And now, with the development of my newfound spiritual connection, these meditations bring even greater joy to me. I can talk with God when I am in need of immediate counsel. It's as though I have a personal friend who is the wisest of the wise, who will drop everything in an instant and favor me with an answer to a tough life question or decision.

When I take time to relax, kick back, and swim in togetherness with the universal Godhead, He ushers me in, quiets me down, and we become of one mind. Each time, I am reborn anew: me a new me, He still and always He, and we always able to be We and yet One at the same time, whenever we want to. It's hard, no, it's *impossible*, to fully explain in words, but even a lifelong Pantheist like I have always been can experience the Universal Love as represented by the Holy Trinity.

Before my healing took place, that special day in my life a couple months ago, I could never accept the seemingly gigantic logical absurdities offered by Christian Theology. The unity of the Holy Spirit, God, the Christ, and their simultaneous individuality, the whole One God yet Three thing … the resurrection, the virgin birth, even the very idea of God as a *being*. Hell's Bells, it's just plain ridiculous *if you think about it*. However, spirituality is not something you can ascend to through the thinking intellect. It is an experience you can have, something you can do, at any time, in any place, under any circumstances. You just have to let go of your "self." Allow your small, isolated, petty little egocentric self to die, and you will be amazed at the truth of your rightful inheritance.

Let me say this right here. I know that many reading this book are not of the Christian faith. Many are of no faith at all. Many actually despise "religion" in any form and not without good reason. After all, more crimes of man against man, more heinous acts of hatred and wanton bloodshed, have been committed in the name of "Allah," or "God," or "Yahweh," than any other cause in recorded history. I do not consider myself in any way a religious person and am appalled beyond measure by the amount of corruption and misrepresentation of true spiritual connection that the churches, cathedrals, mosques, synagogues and temples have perpetuated over the millennia. So, do not misunderstand my intent and meaning when I say I am a Christian. I don't care if you are a Muslim, Hindu, Buddhist, Sikh, Jew, Bahai, agnostic or atheist, I love you with the love of Christ. Spirituality should bring people closer together in love. If your spiritual path is doing that, it is working well. If your path (or no path) is leading you to differentiate and discriminate between people and causing you to withhold your love from "the others," then I say it is *not* working.

This book is about truth. It is intended to help people, help them rid themselves of addiction in all its forms. Religion, with all its man-made rules and societal and cultural discriminations, can be a form of addiction. Crack cocaine was my substance substitute for true inner peace and connection with universal love. Religion can be just as much a drug substitute to any person who needs to connect with the Godhead but instead buys into the rules and regulations, cutting him/herself off from intimacy with the Divine. The scriptures are roadmaps, intended to get you beyond yourself. Do not get addicted to the map. Get to the place where it is pointing … that's the whole point!

Whether God is a being, or a non-being, an energy source, the ultimate "It," the dancer/creator, the Big Bang Man, or all or none of the above is of little concern to me any more. As a thinker, I of course have fun engaging in trying to figure things out. The amazing feature of true scriptural writings is that they ultimately lead you to a place where you must go beyond what you can conceptually grasp. You must take a leap off the cliff of rationality and have faith that the net of truth will be revealed to you and the truth will set you free. You just have to do it, and then you can think about it later, if that's what amuses you.

This leads me to the main point of what I have discovered through this perilous journey. Here is the *essence* of what I have learned and the core of my teaching: In order to be truly free from the inner pain that leads to addictive behavior, you must get to the bottom of who and what you are. There is an ultimate addiction that is pervasive in the human race. We all have it. We all develop it as young children growing up. *We are all addicted to our "selves."* Once you have seen through this illusory and deceptive division between you and all that is, you will realize your divine birthright. At that point, all will be well with you. No need for self-medicating. You will be drunk with the Love of God, so high, no man-made drug could ever come close to delivering the rapture you feel.

Stop clinging to the impermanence of your body and all its clamoring for pleasures of the flesh. Let go of your idea that your thought cycles are really you and originate with you. You are not your own. You belong to the universe. If your body is really you, why can't you control the growth of your hair or stop your fingernails from getting long? If your mind is really you, why can't you control which thoughts come when? Consciousness, the awareness of "I Am" and free will are divine gifts, and our sojourn through this miraculous and awesome plane of existence is what we make it to be through our free-will choices. As you have read, the choices I made led me straight to Hell. A different set of choices, choices that were unselfish, would've led to a far different place and a much better one. Thank God there were unselfish spiritual members of my family who extended their hand of love and concern out to me.

Now I would like to share with you my recipe for living a life that is free of addiction, including freedom from the ultimate addiction to the small isolated self that gets us all into trouble. In everything you do, every deed, thought and action, from the smallest and least-significant, to the largest and most-monumental, follow this hierarchy of priority: Always put God (or whatever you want to refer to IT as) first, family second, *all others* third, and self last. A simple formula and certainly not an original one, I know. As simple as it is, it is equally as difficult to put into practice and adhere to at all times. But it works. It really does.

So much work is left to do, and God willing I live on for a time longer, my remaining life is, and will be, dedicated to trying to get it all done. My wife once asked me, during my rehabilitation, if I felt I would ever be able to be around the drug scene again without fear and danger of relapse. I told her it was my desire, and *aspiration*, to not only be able to be around it, but I intended to *seek it out* and reach out to those poor lost people, helping them in any way I can.

I feel that way today more than ever before; and better yet, I am confident that I am well on the way to being just what the doctor ordered for my wayward brothers and sisters, still wandering through the satanic realms of despair and drug-induced pain relief. I know the agony they are in, from first-hand experience, and my heart will ache for them as long as I live. I've got something to say to them and some much needed good news to share, also.

At this point in my life, I have no specific idea of what my life's work will take form as. I am currently being told to just stay quiet, listen, and be aware, be patient, keep my eyes and ears open for what help is needed, wherever, whenever, and for whomever, do my best to provide it, have faith and trust in Him, and He will take care of me. So that's what I am doing.

Allow me to end this story by closing with a prayer, if you will.

"Be one with me God, and show me your will as I know that you will. I know in my selfishness I have doubted you, felt cheated by you, shouted at you, and abandoned you, and screamed foul language at you, just as you had planned. And I also know you need no reminders from me and have already written these words in the script of my life. You have revealed to me just how one we are and have allowed me to come to the place wherein you can see yourself through me, as a reflection of yourself. Thank you again. And thanksgiving I give to you forever. Amen."

EPiLOGUE

The process of putting my story into words, including having to read it over and over for any necessary editorial changes and/or grammatical corrections, was by and large a much-needed cathartic and healing procedure. But it was brutally painful. The *truth* had to be told, and the truthful story was often excruciating as I read it back, having to somehow identify with and understand this person I was writing about. The task of maintaining absolute honesty in my story was an arduous one, to say the very least. Real, deep, unafraid genuineness and truthfulness about things of the inner heart had never been my forte in life; but I knew that if I were to be healed, and if my story were ever to be helpful to anyone, the taking of the pain was going to be necessary for the gain.

It was difficult for me to write also, because I knew it might be profoundly burdensome for certain loved ones in my life who would eventually be reading the real and whole truth about me, and the details of how I did betray, and how often, and in so many ways had repeatedly betrayed their trust in and love for me. A critical segment of the healing progression for a recovering addict is going back to all those you have betrayed, hurt and wounded through your selfishness and foolishness, and apologizing to them. You must take the heat, allow them to vent, be willing to repent, and make amends humbly, with unabashed emotional, and spiritual, nakedness. You must allow yourself to be vulnerable, and even though you may be fraught with fear, you must do so with fearlessness. There is *no easy way* to do this, yet and still it *must be done.*

In many ways, my story and situation are exceptional. I was lucky. I had a family who cared about me and loved me. I had a stable, loving and spiritual upbringing as a child. I was gifted with an ability to write, reason and reflect. I had helpful and necessary resources become miraculously available, even without any money, to come to my aid, through the selfless giving of family and loved ones. Such fortuitousness is not the norm in the lost world of drug and alcohol addiction.

My heart will ache eternally for the multitudes of wretched castaways, drifting aimlessly and hopelessly through the sea of apathy and loneliness that is their life; devoid of any care or love from anyone, relieving the pain in their tortured, aching souls, by killing themselves, slowly but surely, with a bottle, a needle, or a pipe. I now know from direct experience, what a monumental and Herculean effort is needed to kick a serious addiction. I understand why so very few are ever able to do it, and why it is so rare when relapse *does not* occur. It's hard enough to kick when help *is* available and provided with love. It is next to *impossible* without those elements. Even more imperative, I now know and believe, is the willingness on the addict's part to "give it up" to a higher power.

Although I was initially repulsed and repelled by the AA "12-step" meetings and the fundamental premises and philosophies upon which they operate, I have come around to some measure of agreement with them as a result of my own experience. Those afflicted with serious addictions *are* really powerless to fully tame the beast within, without any help, and by himself or herself. A real and total cure is not possible or lasting if you believe you have the power within your individual self to overcome the demons that possess you and control you. You *need help* to do it, *lots of it*, and the kind of help that is needed is way out of your reach if you are unwilling to admit to the reality of your own inability to do it alone.

That help came to me through accepting God's Grace and developing a personal relationship with Christ. Again, I am not evangelizing here, nor am I putting forth the uncompromising premise that this is the one and only way an individual can fully be cured from his or her addiction. I'm not even saying that it's the only way to connect with God, or whatever you want to call It. It is what worked for me, and I highly recommend it, if you haven't tried it, even if you don't think you need it. *We are all addicts in one way or another,* if we but take the time to honestly evaluate ourselves and measure our state of mind and soulful existence, in comparison with the ideal of perfection. That perfection I have come to call God. Call It what you will, but call *upon* It you must, if you are to be truly free from pain and anxiety.

So I do now agree with my 12-stepping brothers and sisters, that no one is ever able to be permanently free from their addictions, unless he or she admits helplessness to do it alone. Where I still *disagree* with them is that there is no whole and lasting cure for the addict. There is one I know of, for sure. It's called Grace. It is available, it is free, and it is eternal. Nowhere in my deepest meditations, or dreams at night, or dreams of the day, do I experience any more the cravings for crack cocaine that once possessed me. They are gone. They are nothing but a distant memory. And a disgusting memory at that.

The remaining task at hand, is reaching out to the lost world of addiction, helping in any way I can, my beloved lost brothers and sisters, who were, and are, less fortunate than I was and am now. *Please, please, dear reader* ... if you know of anyone who could be helped by the reading of my story; if you can think of someone who in any way might possibly be dissuaded from making (or continuing to make) the mistakes I have made, and avert certain ruin and death, ***please ... give them this book!*** If they cannot read, read it to them. If they cannot feel, feel it *for* them. If they are unable to love themselves, love them *for* them, *just as they are*.

Many are the lessons I've learned as a result of my journey. My beliefs are so much more real and concrete to me now. I used to *theorize* that we are all one, all connected … you know, the whole quantum mechanics/Way of the Tao/ancient mystical teachings/parallel universes/worm holes/atomic particles not really being real "stuff" and yet everywhere at once line of Ultimate It thinking. Good stuff, and very true. Now however, I just *know* we are all one, all connected. Can't really explain it, don't need to. When Jesus says, "Is it not written in your law, ye are gods?" and when He further prays, "That they may all be one, as thou, Father, art in me, and I in thee, that they also may be one in us," I don't have to *believe* this stuff, *I know it.*

As a body, the human race is sick. We are in the emergency room. There is no time or room for apathy, because when one group of cells is "dis-eased," the whole organism is affected. Even if you personally live in a peaceful setting, have no major concerns, and are living the good life in relative serenity, if you do nothing to help stop the spread of the cancer, it will eventually disease you as well, because none of us are separate, or any different, from the sick among us. We're just sick or healthy versions of each other. We're living in one great big lost-and-found room.

Certainly we cannot all be crusaders, and we all have our personal agendas as we act out the melodramas of our selfish little lives, but doing nothing at all to try and better this body is quite simply accepting a slow and sure death. To quote Edward Burrows, "All that is required for evil to prevail, is for good people to do nothing."

We all have to start somewhere. An age-old adage of wisdom says, "The journey of a thousand miles begins with the first step." I have taken the first step and am committed to the journey, 'til death do I part this world. As long as our society and world remains abundant with the lost, the weary, and the needy in spirit, I will not rest, until the last one is saved from the pain of being estranged from God's love. Join hands, and lock arms with me, and with those many wonderful people among us, who love and care, for *all* God's children.

One of those wonderful people is my sister-in-law, named Theresa in my story. To her is dedicated the following poem I wrote one magical morning on the front porch of Camp Shiloh. It will suffice here, as a fitting summary and conclusion.

"A Man, a Word, a Woman, and a Father Once Met"

On the front porch,
before the birds sang the new day awake,
a man sat naked, listening to his heart, listening . . . listening.

Then came a word,
it was heard by the man,
and he was told by the word that the word was to be said,
and told, to all who would listen.

With the advent of a new son-rise, an old cold night gave up the ghost,
and the prance of life revealed itself anew-
another dance, another chance for the old man.

"What shall I do with this new day?" the man asked himself aloud,
and he heard a woman's voice say, "Dance with my Father."
"But what shall I wear, and what gifts shall I bear,

for I am stripped of all possessions and am naked!" he cried.
And he wept, for he was ashamed of his own reflection.
The woman dried his tears, calmed his fears, and said,

"My Father has already seen you naked, and he loves what he sees."
"Now Dance!"

So the man, who had been old,
learned some new steps that morning,
and he stopped his mourning, his pining, and his whining.

He felt suddenly brand new, and to make things even better, he *then* knew
that the woman's Father was *his*, too!
The three of them danced for a full day, and the man told the word he had heard
without thinking about it, to any and all, who knew nothing about it.

The Counselor's Perspective (Written by Pastor Kimberly Linn Wilson)

"***Marvin's addicted to crack!***" The words of my husband were almost vaporous, beyond my grasp. Someone I knew was a crackhead? My mind wandered through puddles of darkness and horrid thoughts of a drug I had seen suck people inside out. Memories erupted of the sickly sweet smell that hit my nostrils whenever I went inside homes I had to visit as a social worker. My clients never smoked it in front of me, they didn't have to; I knew what it was. I saw the effects of it, and they were all too real. I can't remember one positive thought initially; it made me feel ill to think about it.

There was talk, talk within the family, and I kept hearing the shock of the family and their feelings of frustration. Underneath it all, though, there was a current of love that was fathomless. This incredible family was there, with love, and genuine care. Marvin needed rescuing, and the Wilsons were born to do that; it's an innate quality, for even extended family. It's like God commissioned them to rescue the ones who seem beyond rescuing. Their love reached out to Marvin like a light in the darkness, and somewhere, somehow, he found enough strength to reach out and grab the line. They stood on one side of the pit like some old-fashioned tug of war team, and the only person on the other side was Marvin. They were bound and determined, whatever the cost, that he was coming through the sludge, and they were going to pull him across. They'd worry about the cleansing later; the only objective now was to save Marvin.

There was a *lot* of talk. Talk between the brothers, the mother, the wife, and the children. I kept hearing things in a synopsis. They had tried a three-day rehab program, and it didn't work; Marvin had relapsed. Things were getting worse. The family was exasperated and running out of options. My mother-in-law had found a program that had a great success rate; it was a Christian facility, and they would take Marvin for free.

It sounded great to me, but Marvin didn't want to go. He wanted to go to anywhere but there. I thought that was selfish, because someone would have to come up with money for another program. There was also that lingering question, "What if he didn't make it?" I put my two cents in, and reiterated more than a few times, that you don't enable an addict. They needed a place to stash this guy until they could get him into treatment. Our house was logical, because it always has been an emergency room of sorts. My husband and I agreed, after some huge hesitancy on my part, to take his brother in for a three-day stay, until we could get him to this Christian program. I reluctantly agreed to just *three days and no more.*

I lectured my husband that his brother may not be the same person. From what I knew about the drug, it inhaled you and left a shell of a human in your place. After all, crackheads steal, they lie, and they can't be trusted. I arranged to get some kids from the youth group to hang out at our house, just to have more sets of eyes to "watch" my brother-in-law. They could muscle him if necessary. I had mental images of Marvin shoving people out of the way, running out the door and down the street, on a mad dash to get some crack. I didn't trust him, but I didn't want to have to watch him, either. He scared me. I didn't know what to expect, but I was prepared for the worst. Whatever the case, I would only have to tolerate the situation for three days. For me, that was a boundary I felt I could handle. Three days, yeah, I could do that. I figured I would just be polite, and then he'd be on his way, and my life would get back to its normal-abnormal chaos. My son would give up his room and *take all his valuables with him.* It was only three days, just three days. A three-hour tour….

Our dog barked, and I went to the door, knowing they were home. In walked Marvin, ashen and gaunt, a smile of courtesy on his face and a cloud of darkness around him. His head was down most of the time, and he avoided eye contact. We exchanged a few pleasantries, and he went to his room. He was saturated with the smell of crack.

He hung his jacket in the foyer, and it would be weeks before I could walk in or out of the house without smelling that odor. He went to his room, and I went off to do stuff in my office. The first round bell rang somewhere in the distance.

I can't even describe the dark vacuum that I felt in the house. Marvin would be cooking grilled cheese sandwiches, and he'd forget to turn the burner off because his mind was so foggy. I thought about how he might burn the house down. We began talking, and even though I enjoyed our conversations, at the end of my days, I felt like I had given out much more than what I had to give. I started being enveloped by darkness, and I quickly got more depressed than I can remember being in many years. I felt like everything was futile, like there was no point to anything. I told God that if this was what Christianity was all about, He could keep it. I know, I'm feeling all this after just a few days. I'm not a pushover or an ungrounded baby Christian. It was just *that much* of a spiritual battleground for Marvin's life. I felt like I was carrying him on my back, and he was the size of an elephant.

Thoughts rolled around in my head that I'm not proud of. It was part of the journey, and I was going to be exposed to the truth. I figured the whole thing with Marvin's addiction had humbled him, and that this was just providence for him. After all, a man who had rejected the faith of his family, fallen flat on his face, and then gotten rescued through that faith … could be a good thing. I thought the Christian recovery place would be just what he needed, and I was an advocate for that direction. He had left "my" faith, along with his wife and children, and they all needed rescuing. I felt this was God's moment to reach him and his family. Everything was set up, until we hit the third day.

Suddenly, I began hearing about how the family didn't want to send Marvin to a place where he didn't want to go. His behavior was mopey, and he was letting everybody know he was really dreading the Christian "concentration camp." *Who cares where HE wants to go,* I thought. *He has no right to choose the best place; he's made choices that weren't so good.* The alternate place being considered was in California, with a cost of around nine thousand bucks, and the money would have to be borrowed.

"Honey, you can't enable a drug addict," I protested profusely. I was then informed that Marvin's daughter was trying to get a loan, and he wasn't to be told yet. I disagreed and felt that if he knew he would be draining money from his daughter, he would never allow it. I wouldn't do it if I were in his shoes! After all, the Christian program was free and had a huge success rate, even higher than the California program. Why not try the free program, and if it doesn't work, then shell out the money for the other one? The big hitch was there was no detoxification program at the Christian facility. Marvin and his immediate family had read on the Web that crack will stay in your system in the fatty cells and can erupt years after, with some driving need to get high. He felt it absolutely necessary to detoxify his system through medically qualified professionals. I felt like it was just an excuse to avoid the Christian facility and said so many times. I was politely asked to keep my mouth shut, and Marvin was only told that the family was "working on it." I knew he was distressed about going to a Christian facility, and I could only pray. I didn't know what else to do. I just wanted a resolution, and I wanted it fast. Three days would now be seven at the most!

On the seventh day, I was exhausted and entertaining borderline suicidal thought. I felt so drained and empty, but Marvin *was* getting clearer. He still was a bit foggy, but he was much more interactive and social. This day his wife was with us. I thought it incredible that this vibrant African-American woman had stuck by this white hippie and loved him to life. They went with us to our church and heard my husband preach about grace. Both of them had a great time, and something cracked that needed to. There was an unspoken current of judgment that was crumbling on both sides of the wall. I now cared a lot more for this man and was seeing God strip away my judgmental thoughts.

He had been crushed by Christianity as a young man, and the service had stripped away some of that hurt with the saving message of grace. He had been judgmental about Christians. From what I was learning from him, he shared some pretty negative attitudes that I had heard from others outside Christianity. The people who hate Christianity usually don't hate *it*; they hate the people who *represent* it. I've been immature and hated by people who thought I was pushy … I was.

Marvin had written a book that he wanted me to read. It was a unique story about his daughter marrying, and becoming, a Muslim. I didn't want to read it, but he had read my book that was extremely Bible-oriented, and I thought it only fair to read his. My husband had skimmed over it and really didn't give it a rave review. I began reading it reluctantly and then began understanding more about my brother Marvin. I saw a man who left his faith because he felt rejected by it. He seemed to not be able to measure up. He told me he tried to get saved but he couldn't. I thought that was a remarkable statement.

He later told my husband that what he had experienced that Sunday at our church was what he thought Christianity *should* be like and never had been to him. We were embarking on a healing process, together, and I was starting to like it, even if I didn't want to admit it.

The four of us, my husband, Marvin, his wife, and myself, all were meeting after church. I was already prepared to lower the boom. I could not sacrifice myself any longer, and I felt if he stayed, I would not survive. My husband sat there, in anticipation of me laying down the law. Marvin was the first to speak. He sat there so humbled and broken. The past seven days melted away as he spoke, and I felt the presence of God envelop the room. He talked about how blown away he and his wife were at church and that he wanted to help us with the ministry however he could.

He also said he had received grace and felt like he had finally made it home for the first time in his life. The question came, and we were asked if he could stay at our house. When he finished, with tears flowing freely, my husband looked at me. I told Marvin and his wife that we loved and cared about them, and I could not deny the presence of God in the room. I suddenly knew that it was the will of God for him to stay, and that God would help me get through it. I felt a rush of refreshing water enter my soul, and it was done. Marvin would stay.

Shortly after that day, Marvin's wife explained that their family was concerned that he wasn't getting professional counseling. The person who had been overwhelmed before, suddenly opened her mouth, and I committed to being his counselor. We had already been building on that kind of relationship anyway; it's my natural inclination. That's the kind of counsel that's wonderful, where you don't have to think about it, you just do it. Marvin and his wife didn't know about my degree in counseling or my years of experience doing the same. Everyone sighed, and the next stage of our journey was on. I deliberately didn't set a schedule, but we met several times a week, for sometimes two hours, much more intensive than a normal counseling relationship. Marvin made incredible progress, and so did I. I learned God's laws of counsel didn't involve beating people over the head with Jesus. I was cautioned in my heart to not bring up spiritual matters or let them get to the point where I was trying to *teach* him anything. All I had to do was love Marvin, and the doors would just open so easily that I didn't have to try. Our counseling sessions weren't patterned by anybody but God. I liked it better that way.

Marvin and I drew closer and, with the reading of his manuscript, I felt I understood more. Here was this wonderful, compassionate man, who had gone into the world to find "It." He had tasted the different faiths out there and found them wanting in some way. That didn't mean he didn't find good things in them; he just didn't fit fully into them.

He had a higher ideal and couldn't seem to find it anywhere, so he just developed his own idea about things. What a passionate human being! He seemed to me like those people who can't seem to reconcile why God would have His people kill babies. They decide that He's not the kind of God they want to get to know if He's that mean. They just can't get past that one thing, that one catch. Why do people burn in Hell? Why do people suffer? Why, if God is a God of love, does He let bad stuff happen? Why does anyone deserve death, or pain, or bad days? The people who accept God on blind faith don't seem to struggle with these questions; they can just believe. The more analytical cannot reconcile questions they have, and many intellectuals do not embrace Christianity for that reason. Marvin seemed to be one of those people, but now things were different.

I watched walls fall down, and both Marvin and I had several weeks of illuminations. Marvin was reconciling his faith with his experience of it, and I was experiencing a new understanding of mine. As we grew, our counseling time became moments of joy for both of us, and we'd laugh and cry in our times together. I remember one poignant moment when Marvin dug into his box of belongings and pulled out two letters. I read them both to Marvin, as he listened. One was from him to his father, as a young man in his 20's, explaining why he was becoming a Buddhist. It was full of his hurt and frustration, and the desire for his father to be proud of him. The whole letter seemed to be a struggle and came out of a heart that seemed to be in the midst of searching. The other letter was from Marvin's dad. He had been a Pastor for many years, and it was full of grace and wisdom; we both wept as I read it out loud. We figured out that his dad would've been about Marvin's age now, back when he had written it. The years between them seemed to fade away, as Marvin met his dad in this moment in time. His father had passed away seven years ago, but the words were prophetic. These words are so powerful and intimate, but I believe you will see the deep character of Christ in Marvin's father, as you read them.

"I committed you to the Lord at your birth, and am perfectly content to leave you with Him now."

"I do daily ask Him to lead you to where, and to be what He wants you to be, and do."

"I believe that the Lord spared your life, and gave you health, because he had, and has, a place for you. While I do not know what that is, I do pray that you will be led to that place."

It was a powerful day, and it really felt like a welcome-home letter to me. It was like his father had seen him from afar off and just somehow knew that his faith would carry on beyond his death and see his son find the fullness that he had been looking for. Oh, what an awesome and inspiring faith to believe in God, that your children will find peace, even if it's after your death! I only wish I could've known him better; what a great man of God.

I went through a transformation of my own, as I saw the darkness of my own heart. It's so easy to get into the "us" and "them" camp mentality as Christians. No wonder the world struggles with the examples in our faith. I've had people tell me they don't want to wait on people who are Christians, because they don't tip as much. Christians have a reputation of complaining, and I used to see it in my friends from church. They gave the waitresses and waiters such a hard time that I was embarrassed. They'd even get the lunch buffet, stay until the afternoon, and eat again before they left! I guess we have some work to do. My own issues weren't any better. I didn't say very nice things about people with differing political views, Muslims, or even some of my fellow Christians, for that matter.

One day we were in the car, going somewhere, Marvin was driving, and I confessed that I had gotten all caught up in the political thing during the last election. I told him how convicted I got, because it caused me to choose a side and almost hate anyone with an opposing view. I had since realized that Jesus would not choose political sides or hate anyone who did. It was one of many heart changes for me.

I also realized that God could take someone through whatever journey He wanted to. We are so judgmental about what people are doing that we forget to love, love, LOVE! How in the world do we expect people to come to Christ when we are terrible representatives of His grace? It's the walls we put up, regarding people of other faith, form or fashion, that cause us to not witness the love of God. Jesus had this incredible way of seeing *people*, not religion, not race, not sin. He just loved people and led them to the truth. I was learning to do that with Marvin. I just loved him and talked to him as a friend, and God is the one who changed him.

Our counseling sessions were transparent. If there was something I felt in my heart to share about myself, I did. If I had a question to ask, no matter how raw it was, I asked. I also had to brace myself for impact, because Marvin would let it fly occasionally, and words would come out that offended my sensibilities. Yes, they bothered me, but I had to love past my inability to hear those things and just listen to the heart of what he was saying. The most powerful counsel is reciprocal, both of you growing from each other in grace, truth and love. If a counselor is unwilling to be transparent in order to help someone, then I don't believe the counseling will be as effective.

God used this broken, hurting man, to teach me that He loves everyone, regardless of what they've been through or who they think they are. We have to stop judging in the body of Christ, because God's gifts are without repentance. God had to make them that way, because we're imperfect people trying to serve a perfect God. We tend to choose the rules and regulations over *people*.

I saw Marvin go from getting clean to getting involved, to being on our praise and worship team, to teaching people how to play guitar. Five years ago, I would've demanded he be clean and go through cleansing classes and all sorts of other hoops, before he could play in the praise band. Now, God has shown me the error of my ways.

We all sin, and you can't say one sin is worse than the other; they all separate us from God. My mentor would say, "There is no such thing as a perfect church, so we might as well have church." Since this new revelation, our church has grown, we've grown, and Marvin has remained on this powerful journey.

I'm glad Marvin came into my life. I'm thankful for the journey it set me on, to expose my heart and its need for more love and acceptance. I absolutely love my brother Marvin with all my heart, and I know he has so much to share with the body of Christ. I'm excited to see all the music, books, love and joy he is going to add to us. *I wonder how many more people are out there who just need the support and love* to come into an understanding of who they can be in Christ. My world is a better place for knowing Marvin. Thanks so much for Marvin, Jesus!

BIBLIOGRAPHY

1. According to the 1972 National Committee on Marijuana and Drug Use (MCMDU), more than 60 percent of all college students had used marijuana, and of those ages 15 to 20 who had not attained any college education, 84 percent had used marijuana.

2. Facts taken from "An interview with Alfred McCoy," 1990, by David Barsamian. This interview with Alfred McCoy took place while McCoy was steeped in research for, and writing, his second book, **The Politics of Heroin; *CIA Complicity In The Global Drug Trade*.** Alfred W. McCoy is professor of Southeast Asian History at the University of Wisconsin, Madison. Educated at Columbia and Yale.

3. Data taken from the 2003 FOA (Food and Agricultural Organization of the United Nations) "World Drink Trends" report.

4. Data taken from the 2001 survey on national drug abuse by SAMHSA (Substance Abuse and Mental Health Services Administration).

5. Data taken from the report: "Violence Against Women" organized by UN Division for the Advancement of Women in collaboration with ECE and WHO, 11-14 April, 2005, in Geneva, Switzerland.

6. Data obtained from: Watts, C, Zimmerman C. Violence Against Women: global scope and magnitude. Lancet, 2002, 359:1232-1237.

About The Author

Marvin Wilson is the son of a Christian minister, a family man, husband, father, and grandfather. He has had several professional careers, including: musician, nightclub entertainer, construction contractor, Buddhist minister, network marketer, motivational speaker, sales trainer, and adult education teacher. Marvin considers his life to be a spiritual journey, and each of life's experiences, whether troublesome or pleasurable, to be lessons. Teachings from God. Throughout his entire adult life, he has been journal keeper, a reflective writer about these lessons, and the attendant wisdom and understanding gained through experiencing them.

The most significant and painful lesson Marvin has ever endured and lived through was his complete economic, emotional, psychological, and spiritual downfall in his mid-fifties. This experience was nearly fatal, as it culminated in a serious narcotics addiction. The lessons learned about humility, faithfulness, integrity, genuineness and honesty, and putting God first, others second, and self last, in every situation, however challenging and difficult to understand, are the foundation and basis for his decision to publish his first book, entitled *I Romanced The Stone.*

Visit Marvin at www.rockofallages.com.

LaVergne, TN USA
04 December 2009
166018LV00002B/32/A

9 780977 968039